Reverse Mortgages

How to Use Reverse Mortgages to Secure Your Retirement

Julian Ashford

ISBN: 9781807650513

Published by TPSA Publishing

Table of Contents

INTRODUCION

Reverse mortgages are often dismissed with a quick wave of the hand—too expensive, too risky, too complicated, or simply "not for people like me." That reputation has kept many retirees and near-retirees from seriously evaluating a financial tool that can, in the right circumstances, strengthen retirement security and flexibility.

This book is written for homeowners who want to make clear, confident decisions about how home equity fits into a retirement income plan. A reverse mortgage is not a magic solution, and it is not appropriate for everyone. But it can be a powerful way to coordinate housing wealth with other retirement resources—especially when the real challenge of retirement begins: turning a lifetime of savings into income that must last for an unknown number of years.

We will start with the foundations of retirement income planning and the key risks retirees face—longevity, market volatility, inflation, spending shocks, and cognitive decline—then connect those ideas to the housing decisions that shape retirement life. From there, you'll learn the background and history of reverse mortgages, how they work in practice, what eligibility and costs look like, and why features such as the growing line of credit can matter more than most people realize.

We will also compare reverse mortgages with alternatives like HELOCs, address tax considerations, and clarify repayment realities so you can separate facts from common misconceptions. Most importantly, the focus here is strategy. You'll explore practical uses for reverse mortgages, including coordinating withdrawals, supporting sustainable spending, improving portfolio resilience, and protecting the home's value—so you can evaluate whether, when, and how a reverse mortgage may contribute to a responsible retirement plan.

By the end, you should have a framework to ask better questions, avoid costly mistakes, and decide with clarity—whether you ultimately choose to use a reverse mortgage or not. ì

CHAPTER 1: OVERVIEW OF RETIREMENT INCOME PLANNING

Without the relative stability provided by earnings from employment, retirees must find a way to convert their financial resources into a stream of income that will last the remainder of their lives. Two trends add to the difficulty of this task. First, people are living longer, and those retiring in their sixties must plan to support a longer period of spending. Second, traditional defined-benefit pensions are becoming less common. Pensions once guaranteed lifetime income by pooling risks across a large number of workers, but fewer employees have access to them today. Instead, employees and employers now tend to contribute to various defined-contribution pensions like 401(k)s where the employee accepts longevity and investment risk and must make investment decisions. 401(k) plans are not pensions in the traditional sense, as they shift the risks and responsibilities to employees.

If you've been saving and accumulating, the question remains about what to do with your pot of assets on reaching retirement. Essentially, if you wish to retire one day, you are increasingly responsible to figure out how to save during your working years and convert your savings into sustainable income for an ever-lengthening number of retirement years. It is not an easy task, but it is manageable.

My goal is to help guide you along the right path to building an efficient retirement income strategy. Ultimately, this is something you may seek to do on your own, but as an informed consumer of the financial services profession, I will also offer suggestions on how to obtain help if you decide to seek further assistance.

It is important to note from the outset that retirement income planning is still a relatively new field. Wealth management has traditionally focused on accumulating assets without applying further thought to the differences that happen after retirement. To put it succinctly, retirees experience reduced capacity to bear financial market risk once they have retired. The standard of living for a retiree becomes more vulnerable to enduring permanent harm as a result of financial market downturns.

While it is relatively new, retirement income planning has emerged as a distinct field in the financial services profession. It continues to suffer from growing pains as it gains recognition, but increased research and brainpower in the field have benefited those planning for retirement and retirees alike. It is now clear that the financial circumstances facing retirees are not the same as pre-retirees, calling for different approaches from traditional investment advice for wealth accumulation.

A mountain climbing analogy is useful for clarifying the distinction between accumulation and distribution, as the ultimate goal of climbing a mountain is not just to make it to the top, it is also necessary to get back down. The skillset required to get down a mountain is not the same as that needed to reach the summit. In fact, an experienced mountain climber knows that it is more treacherous and dangerous to climb down a mountain. On the way down, climbers must deal with greater fatigue, they risk falling farther and with greater acceleration when facing a downslope compared to an upslope, and the way our bodies are designed makes going up easier than coming down.

Distribution—the retirement phase when you are pulling money from your accounts rather than accumulating wealth—is much like descending a mountain. The objective of a retirement saver is not just to make it to the top of the mountain, which we could view as achieving a wealth accumulation target. The real objective is to safely and smoothly make it down the mountain, spending assets in a sustainable manner for as long as you live.

The Retirement Researcher Manifesto

As I have attempted to summarize the key messages and themes that have underscored my writing and research going into this book, I find the following eight guidelines serve as a manifesto for my approach to retirement income planning. Much of my writing concerns how to implement these guidelines into a retirement income plan.

1. Play the long game. A retirement income plan should be based on planning to live, not planning to die. A long life will be expensive to support, and it should take precedence over death planning. Fight the impatience that could lead you to choose short-term expediencies carrying greater long-term cost. This does not mean, however, that you sacrifice short-term satisfactions to plan for the long-term. Many efficiencies can be gained from a long-term focus that can support a higher sustained standard of living for as long as you live.

You still have to plan for a long life, even when rejecting strategies that only help in the event of a long life. Remember, planning for average life expectancy is quite risky—half of the population outlives their expectancy. Planning to live longer means spending less than otherwise. Developing a plan that incorporates efficiencies that will not be realized until later can allow more spending today in anticipation of those efficiencies. Not taking such long-term, efficiency-improving actions will lead to a permanently reduced standard of living.

Some strategies I have discussed that focus on building a long-term plan over accepting short-term expediencies include the following:

- delaying the start of Social Security benefits,

- purchasing income annuities,

- paying a bit more taxes today in order to enjoy more substantial tax reductions in the future,

- making home renovations and living arrangements with the idea of aging in place,

- planning for the risk of cognitive decline that will make it harder to manage your finances with age, and

- opening a line of credit with a reverse mortgage.

These strategies may not make much sense if the planning horizon is only a couple of years, but they may make a great deal of sense for someone building a sustainable long-term retirement income plan.

2. Do not leave money on the table. The holy grail of retirement income planning is finding strategies that enhance retirement efficiency. I define efficiency as such: if one strategy simultaneously allows for more lifetime spending and a greater legacy value for assets relative to another strategy, then it is more efficient. Efficiency must be defined from the perspective of how long you live. Related to point (1), there can be a number of strategies that enhance efficiency over the long-term (but not necessarily over the short term) with more spending and more legacy. One simple example for tax planning in retirement is taking IRA distributions or harvesting capital gains to generate enough income to fill the 0% marginal tax bracket.

3. Use reasonable expectations for portfolio returns. A key lesson for long-term financial planning is that you should not expect to earn the average historical market returns for your portfolio. Half of the time, realized returns will be less. As well, we have been experiencing a period of historically low interest rates, which unfortunately provides a clear mathematical reality that at least bond returns are going to be lower in the future. This has important implications for those who have retired (these implications are relevant for those far from retirement as well, but the harm of ignoring them is less than for retirees). At the very least, dismiss any retirement projection based on 8% or 12% returns, as the reality is likely much less when we account for portfolio volatility, inflation, a desire to develop a plan that will work more than half the time and in today's low interest rates. As a corollary to this point, while low interest rates generally make retirement more expensive, there are some

strategies that are made more attractive by low interest rates, such as delaying Social Security or opening a reverse mortgage.

4. Be careful about plans that only work with high market returns.

A natural mathematical formula that applies to retirement planning is that higher assumed future market returns imply higher sustainable spending rates. Bonds provide a fixed rate of return when held to maturity, and stocks potentially offer a higher return than bonds as a reward for their additional risk. But a "risk premium" is not guaranteed and may not materialize. Retirees who spend more today because they are planning for higher market returns than available for bonds are essentially "amortizing their upside." They are spending more today than justified by bond investments, based on an assumption that higher returns in the future will make up the difference and justify the higher spending rate.

For retirees, the fundamental nature of risk is the threat that poor market returns trigger a permanently lower standard of living. Retirees must decide how much risk to their lifestyle they are willing to accept. Assuming that a risk premium on stocks will be earned and spending more today is risky behavior. It may be reasonable behavior for the more risk tolerant among us, but it is not a behavior that will be appropriate for everyone. It is important to think through the consequences in advance.

5. Build an integrated strategy to manage various retirement risks. Building a retirement income strategy is a process that requires a determination for how to best combine available retirement income tools in order to meet retirement goals and to effectively protect against the risks standing in the way of those goals. Retirement risks include longevity and an unknown planning horizon, market volatility and macroeconomic risks, inflation and spending shocks that can derail a budget. Each of these risks must be managed by combining different income tools with different relative strengths and weaknesses for addressing each of the risks. There is no single solution that can cover every risk, though some financial products have been marketed as such.

6. Approach retirement income tools with an agnostic view. The financial services profession is generally divided between two camps: those focusing on investment solutions and those focusing on insurance solutions. Both sides have their adherents who see little use for the other side. But the most efficient retirement strategies require an integration of both investments and insurance. It is potentially harmful to dismiss subsets of retirement income tools without a thorough investigation of their purported role. In this regard, it is wrong to describe the stock market as a casino, to lump income annuities together with every other type of annuity, and to dismiss reverse mortgages without any further consideration.

For the two camps in the financial services profession, it is natural to accuse the opposite camp of having conflicts of interest that bias their advice, but each side must reflect on whether their own conflicts color their advice. On the insurance side, the natural conflict is that an insurance agent receives commissions for selling insurance products and only needs to meet a requirement that their suggestions are suitable for their clients. On the investments side, those charging for a percentage of assets they manage naturally wish to make the investment portfolio as large as possible, which is not necessarily in the best interests of their clients who are seeking sustainable lifetime income and proper retirement risk management. Meanwhile, those charging hourly fees for planning advice naturally do not wish to make their recommendations so simple that it foregoes the need for an ongoing planning relationship. It is important to overcome these hurdles and to rely carefully on what the math and research show. This requires starting from a fundamentally agnostic position.

7. Start with the household balance sheet. A retirement plan involves more than just financial assets. The household balance sheet is the starting point for building a retirement income strategy. This has been a fundamental lesson from various retirement frameworks, such as Jason Branning and M. Ray Grubbs' Modern Retirement Theory, Russell Investments' Funded Ratio approach and the Household Balance Sheet view of the Retirement Income Industry Association. At the core of these different methodologies is a desire to treat the household retirement problem in the same way that pension funds treat their obligations. Assets should be matched to liabilities with comparable levels of risk. This matching can either be done on a balance sheet level, using the present values of asset and liability streams, or it can be accomplished on a period-by-period basis to match assets to ongoing spending needs. Structuring the retirement income problem in this way makes it easier to keep track of the different aspects of the plan and to make sure that each liability has a funding source. This also allows a retiree to more easily determine whether they have sufficient assets to meet their retirement needs, or if they may be underfunded with respect to their goals. This organizational framework also serves as a foundation for deciding on an appropriate asset allocation and for seeing clearly how different retirement income tools fit into an overall plan.

Exhibit 1.2 provides a basic overview of potential assets and liabilities on the household balance sheet.

Exhibit 1.2 The Basic Household Balance Sheet

Household Balance Sheet	
Assets	**Liabilities**
Human Capital	Fixed Expenses
Continuing Career	Basic Living Needs
Part-time work	Taxes
	Debt Repayment
Home Equity	
	Discretionary Expenses
Financial Assets	Travel & Leisure
Checking Accounts	Lifestyle Improvements
Brokerage Accounts	
Retirement Plans	Contingencies
	Long-Term Care
Insurance & Annuities	Health Care
	Other Spending Shocks
Social Capital	
Social Security	Legacy Goals
Medicare	Family
Company Pensions	Community & Society
Family & Community	

8. Distinguish between technical liquidity and true liquidity. An important implication from the household balance sheet view is that the nature of liquidity in a retirement income plan must be carefully considered. In a sense, an investment portfolio is a liquid asset, but some of its liquidity may be only an illusion. Assets must be matched to liabilities. Some, or even all, of the investment portfolio may be earmarked to meet future lifestyle spending goals. Curtis Cloke describes this in his Thrive University program for financial advisors (which I have attended twice) as allocation liquidity. A retiree is free to reallocate their assets in any way they wish, but the assets are not truly liquid because they must be preserved to meet the spending goal. While a retiree could decide to use these assets for another purpose, doing so would jeopardize the ability to meet future spending. In this sense, assets are not as liquid as they appear.

This is different from free-spending liquidity, in which assets could be spent in any desired way because they are not earmarked to meet existing liabilities. True liquidity emerges when there are excess assets remaining after specifically setting aside what is needed to meet all of the household liabilities. This distinction is important because there could be cases when tying up part of one's assets in something illiquid, such as an income annuity, may allow for the household liabilities to be covered more cheaply than could be done when all assets are positioned to provide technical liquidity. In simple terms, an income annuity that pools longevity risk may allow lifetime spending to be met at a cost of twenty years of the spending objective, while self-funding for longevity may require setting aside enough from an investment portfolio to cover thirty to forty years of expenses. Because risk pooling and mortality credits allow for less to be set aside to cover the spending goal, there is now greater true liquidity and therefore more to cover other unexpected contingencies without jeopardizing core-spending needs. Liquidity, as it is traditionally defined in securities markets, is of little value as a distinct goal in a long-term retirement income plan.

The Retirement Income Challenge

The process of building a retirement income strategy involves determining how to best combine retirement income tools to optimize the balance between meeting various retirement goals and effectively protecting your goals from retirement risks. Building an optimal strategy is a process, and there is no single right answer. No one approach or retirement income product works best for everyone. Different people will approach the problem in different ways, as some will feel affinity for solutions connected with managing withdrawals from an investment portfolio, while others will begin from a desire to build income guarantees. The objective becomes to flesh out the details for how each income tool could contribute, quantify the advantages and disadvantages of different strategies, and determine how to best combine the income tools into an overall plan.

Possible goals are listed in the next concentric circle. The third circle lists risks confronting those goals. The final outside circle shows available income tools for building a retirement income plan. Much of what follows in this chapter is about fleshing out the details of this exhibit.

Financial Goals for Retirement

It is important to clarify the goals for a retirement-income plan, as different income tools are better suited for different goals. Retirement plans should be customized to each person's specific circumstances. Each retiree should seek to meet specific financial goals in a way that best manages the wide variety of risks that threaten those goals. The primary financial goal for most retirees relates to their spending: maximize spending power (lifestyle) in such a way that spending can remain consistent and sustainable without any drastic reductions, no matter how long the retirement lasts (longevity). Other important goals may include leaving assets for subsequent generations (legacy), and maintaining sufficient reserves for unexpected contingencies that have not been earmarked for other purposes (liquidity). Lifestyle, Longevity, Legacy, and Liquidity are the 4 L's of retirement income.

Changing Risks in Retirement

It is important to understand from the very outset how changing risks are primarily what separate retirement income planning from traditional wealth management. Retirees have less capacity for risk as they become more vulnerable to a reduced standard of living when risks manifest. Those entering retirement are crossing the threshold into an entirely foreign way of living. These risks can be summarized into seven general categories.

1. Reduced Earnings Capacity

Retirees face reduced flexibility to earn income in the labor markets as a way to cushion their standard of living from the impact of poor market returns. One important distinction in retirement is that people often experience large reductions in their risk capacity as the value of their human capital declines. As a result, they are left with fewer options for responding to poor portfolio returns.

Risk capacity is the ability to endure a decline in portfolio value without experiencing a substantial decline in your standard of living. Prior to retirement, poor market returns might be counteracted with a small increase in the savings rate, a brief retirement delay, or even a slight increase in risk taking. Once retired, however, people can find it hard to return to the labor force and are more likely to live on fixed budgets.

2. Visible Spending Constraint

At one time, investments were a place for saving and accumulation, but retirees must try to create an income stream from their existing assets—an important constraint on their investment decisions. Taking distributions amplifies investment risks (market volatility, interest rate volatility, and credit risk) by increasing the importance of the order of investment returns in retirement.

It can be difficult to reduce spending in response to a poor market environment. Portfolio losses could have a more significant impact on standard of living after retirement, necessitating greater care and vigilance in response to portfolio volatility. Even a person with high risk tolerance (the ability to stomach market volatility comfortably) would be constrained by their risk capacity.

The traditional goal of wealth accumulation is generally to seek the highest returns possible in order to maximize wealth, subject to your risk tolerance. Taking on more risk before retirement can be justified because many people have greater risk capacity at that time and can focus more on their risk tolerance. However, the investing problem fundamentally changes in retirement.

Investing during retirement is a rather different matter from investing for retirement, as retirees worry less about maximizing risk-adjusted returns and worry more about ensuring that their assets can support their spending goals for the remainder of their lives. After retiring, the fundamental objective for investing is to sustain a living standard while spending down assets over a finite but unknown length of time. Furthermore, the spending needs that will eventually be financed by the portfolio still reside in the distant future. In this new retirement calculus, views about how to balance the tradeoffs between upside potential and downside protection can change. Retirees might find that the risks associated with seeking return premiums on risky assets loom larger than before, and they might be prepared to sacrifice more potential upside growth to protect against the downside risks of being unable to meet spending objectives.

The requirement to sustain an income from a portfolio is a new constraint on investing that is not considered by basic wealth maximization approaches such as portfolio diversification and Modern Portfolio Theory (MPT). In MPT, cash flows are ignored and the investment horizon is limited to a single, lengthy period. This simplification guides investing theory for wealth accumulation. When spending from a portfolio, the concept of sequence of returns risk becomes more relevant as portfolio losses early in retirement will increase the percentage of remaining assets withdrawn to sustain an income. This can dig a hole from which it becomes increasingly difficult to escape, as portfolio returns must exceed the growing withdrawal percentage to prevent further portfolio depletion. Even if markets subsequently recover, the retirement portfolio cannot enjoy a full recovery. The sustainable withdrawal rate from a retirement portfolio can fall well below the average return earned by the portfolio during retirement.

3. Heightened Investment Risk

As we just discussed, retirees experience heightened vulnerability to sequence of returns risk when they begin spending from their investment portfolio. Poor returns early in retirement can push the sustainable withdrawal rate well below that which is implied by long-term average market returns.

The financial market returns experienced near your retirement date matter a great deal more than you may realize. Retiring at the beginning of a bear market is incredibly dangerous. The average market return over a thirty-year period could be quite generous, but if negative returns are experienced in the early stages when you have started spending from your portfolio, withdrawals can deplete wealth rapidly, leaving a much smaller remainder to benefit from any subsequent market recovery, even with the same average returns over a long period of time.

The dynamics of sequence risk suggest that a prolonged recessionary environment early in retirement without an accompanying economic catastrophe could jeopardize the retirement prospects for particular groups of retirees. Some could experience much worse retirement outcomes than those retiring a few years earlier or later. It is nearly impossible to see such an instance coming, as devastation for a group of retirees is not necessarily preceded or accompanied by devastation for the overall economy.

4. Unknown Longevity

The fundamental risk for retirement is unknown longevity, which is summarized in the question "How long will your retirement plan need to generate income?" The length of your retirement could be much shorter or longer than the statistical life expectancy. A long life is wonderful, but it is also costlier and a bigger drain on resources. Half of the population will outlive their statistical life expectancy, and that number is only increasing as scientific progress constantly increases the number of years we can expect to live. For many retirees, the fear of outliving resources may exceed the fear of death.

5. Spending Shocks

Unexpected expenses come in many forms, including:

- Unforeseen need to help family members,
- Divorce,
- Changes in tax laws or other public policy,
- Changing housing needs,
- Home repairs,
- Rising health care and prescription costs, and
- Long-term care.

Retirees must preserve flexibility and liquidity to manage unplanned expenses. When attempting to budget over a long retirement period, it is important to include allowances for such contingencies.

6. Compounding Inflation

Retirees face the risk that inflation will erode the purchasing power of their savings as they progress through retirement. Low inflation may not be noticeable in the short term, but it can have a big impact over a lengthy retirement, leaving retirees vulnerable. Even with just 3% average annual inflation, the purchasing power of a dollar will fall by more than half after twenty-five years, doubling the cost of living.

Sequence of returns risk is amplified by greater portfolio volatility, yet many retirees cannot afford to play it too safe. Short-term fixed income securities might struggle to provide returns that exceed inflation, causing these assets to be quite risky in a different sense: they may not be able to support a retiree's long-term spending goals. The low-volatility assets are generally viewed as less risky, but this may not be the case when the objective is to sustain spending over a long time horizon. Even low levels of inflation can create dramatic impacts on purchasing power over a long period of time. Retirees must keep an eye on the long-term cumulative impacts of even low inflation and position their assets accordingly.

7. Declining Cognitive Abilities

Finally, a retirement income plan must incorporate the unfortunate reality that many retirees will experience declining cognitive abilities, which will hamper portfolio management and other financial decision-making skills. For the afflicted, it will become increasingly difficult to make sound portfolio investments and withdrawal decisions in advanced ages.

In addition, many households do not equally share the management of personal finances. When the spouse who manages the finances dies first, the surviving spouse can run into serious problems without a clear plan in place. The surviving spouse can be left vulnerable to financial predators and other financial mistakes. Survivors often become more exposed to fraud and theft.

While liquidity and flexibility are important, retirees should also prepare for the reality that cognitive decline will hamper the portfolio management skills of many as they age, increasing the desirability of having an advanced plan locked into place.

Retirement Income Tools

Retirement plans can be built to manage varying risks by strategically combining different retirement income tools. As a result, retirement income planning is now emerging as a distinct field.

Total Return Investment Portfolios

Making systematic withdrawals from a well-diversified investment portfolio is a common way to obtain retirement income. Systematic withdrawals do not protect a retiree from longevity risk or sequence of returns risk, and may only protect from inflation risk when asset returns can keep up with inflation. This approach has its benefits, such as the potential to keep your nest egg growing so you can leave a large inheritance, as well as a sense of technical liquidity that could become true liquidity if markets perform well. A total returns approach is particularly vulnerable to declining cognitive abilities as it requires complex financial decision-making to manage distributions and investments.

Individual Bonds

Leaving behind the purely total returns perspective, another viable option is to hold fixed income assets to their maturity to guarantee upcoming retiree expenses. Often, this will be done to support short-and/or medium-term spending, with a more aggressive investment portfolio with higher expected returns to be deployed for expenses in the long term.

Holding bonds to their maturity can keep you from selling them at a loss, which helps alleviate sequence of returns risk. Individual bonds do not provide longevity protection, however. While they may provide technical liquidity, selling them early to use for other contingencies could result in capital losses as well as the loss of assets that had been earmarked to cover future spending. Traditional bonds will be exposed to inflation risk, but Treasury Inflation-Protected Securities (TIPS) can be used to lock-in the purchasing power of money in real terms.

As for the risk of declining cognitive abilities, managing the bond and investment portfolio may still be complicated, but the bonds can provide additional behavioral benefits. Knowing that income is accounted for over the next several years can help retirees stay the course and not sell off their stock positions in a panic after a market decline. Retirees can take comfort in the knowledge that there will be time for their stocks to recover before they must be sold. By using bonds to provide income for a fixed number of years, it may also be easier for retirees to understand why the overall asset allocation is what it is. Individuals may not be clear why their portfolio has 60% stock funds and 40% bond funds, but if they instead think in terms of how building a bond ladder with 40% of their assets allows for eight years of income, for instance, then the nature of their asset allocation choice may be clearer.

Income Annuities, Traditional Pensions, and Other Annuity Types

Partially annuitizing your assets can also provide an effective way to build an income floor for retirement. Income annuities, as opposed to individual bonds, provide longevity protection by hedging the risks associated with not knowing how long you will live. Fixed annuities can be real or nominal, and the initial payments can begin within one year (single-premium immediate annuities or SPIAs), or be deferred to a later age (deferred income annuities, or DIAs). Some employers still offer traditional defined-benefit pensions, which can also be treated as an income annuity. Though income annuities only represent about 4% of total annuity sales, they are the type of annuity that is of the utmost importance as a retirement income tool.

Deciding whether to annuitize, when to annuitize, how much to annuitize, and whether to build a ladder of annuities over time are all important questions. Annuities protect from longevity and sequence of returns risk, and they can protect from inflation risk if a real annuity is purchased. Because income continues automatically, they also provide protection for cognitive decline. David Laibson, a professor at Harvard University, refers to income annuities as "dementia insurance." They help manage many risks, but they provide no growth potential, and life-only versions will not support an inheritance by themselves. In general, they are also not liquid if more funds are needed for unplanned contingencies. However, partial annuitization combined with investments can be an effective way to create true liquidity on the balance sheet.

Income annuities represent only a small percentage of total annuity sales. Countless types of annuities can be used for many different purposes. Fixed deferred annuities can act as an alternative to CDs or savings accounts; investment-only deferred variable annuities can provide a source of tax-deferred savings during the accumulation phase; and fixed indexed annuities (a newer name for equity indexed annuities), immediate variable annuities, and deferred variable annuities with guarantee riders can all provide various combinations of guaranteed income, liquidity, and upside growth potential. Related non-annuity investment options include the ability to have an income guarantee rider on an investment portfolio, and using financial derivatives to generate the same types of outcomes as some types of annuities on your own.

Social Security

Social Security is the ultimate form of an income annuity, and it is generally one of the largest assets on the household balance sheet. For a high-earning couple, the present value of future Social Security benefits could exceed one million dollars. Social Security provides protection from inflation, longevity, and sequence of returns risk, as well as providing survivor benefits. Retirement benefits can begin as early as age sixty-two, but the benefits grow through age seventy if you wait. If you view lost benefits from ages sixty-two to sixty-nine as a premium to buy a larger annuity starting at seventy, delaying Social Security can be viewed as the best annuity money can buy. It offers a better deal than any commercial providers. Because Social Security income continues automatically over time, it also provides protections for cognitive decline. The only risk Social Security does not help manage is spending shock, as you cannot borrow against your future benefits to obtain greater liquidity today.

Housing Wealth

The other major asset for most households, outside of investment portfolios and Social Security, is home equity, or housing wealth. Housing wealth can be used in a variety of ways in retirement. If care is taken to choose housing that will allow for aging in place, then housing can provide inflation protection and some protection for the uncertain costs related to long-term care. With cognitive or long-term care needs, housing could be used to put off institutional living, and then housing wealth could be redeployed to cover the costs of institutional living when it becomes necessary. With a reverse mortgage, home equity can become a liquid buffer asset which can help serve to reduce exposure to sequence of returns risk, or to cover unexpected contingencies.

Long-Term Care Planning

One of the largest spending shocks facing a retired household is the need for ongoing long-term care. A retirement income plan must account for this, and various tools are available to help control the impacts of long-term care costs on family wealth.

The four main options for meeting long-term care needs include:

- self-funding,

- Medicaid,

- traditional long-term care insurance,

- and new hybrid insurance products that combine long-term care coverage with an annuity or life insurance.

Planning in advance for long-term care needs can help control the impact of spending shocks and cognitive decline.

Other Assets, Insurance, and Income Sources

A hodgepodge of other retirement income tools can also be a valuable source of support for retirement. Decisions made about Medicare or other health insurance can help mitigate the risks of large health care spending shocks throughout retirement. Part-time work, to the extent that it is feasible, can help support a more fulfilling lifestyle while also providing as source of income to help mitigate risks related to market returns. An active mind may also help to limit the onset of cognitive difficulties.

Another source of support is social capital: the ability to obtain help from family members, the community, and the social safety net. Access to these opportunities can help mitigate harms related to the various retirement risks. Other potential assets that are less exposed to market risk and may be available to support retirement goals include life insurance, business holdings, and rental income from real estate.

Insurance vs. Investments

As I mentioned before, retirement income planning has emerged as a distinct field in the financial services profession. But due in part to its relatively new status, the best approach for building a retirement income plan remains elusive. Two fundamentally different philosophies for retirement income planning—which I call "probability-based" and "safety-first"—diverge on the critical issue of where a retirement plan is best served: in the risk/reward tradeoffs of an equity portfolio, or the contractual guarantee of insurance products. The fundamental question asks which type of strategy can best meet the retirement income challenge of combining retirement income tools to meet goals and manage risks.

Those favoring investments (the probability-based) rely on the notion that the market will eventually provide favorable returns for most retirees. Though stock markets are volatile, stocks can be expected to outperform bonds over a reasonable amount of time. The investments crowd considers upside potential from a portfolio to be so significant that insurance solutions can only play a minimal role. Why needlessly cut off the upside? In addition, the investments side feels a general unease about relying on the long-term prospects of insurance companies or bond issuers to meet contractual obligations. Perhaps not fully understanding the implications of how sequence of returns risk differs from market risk, the probability-based school believes that in the rare event that the performance for the equity portfolio does not materialize, an economic catastrophe would sink insurance companies as well.

Meanwhile, those favoring insurance (safety-first) believe contractual guarantees to be reliable and that staking your retirement income on the assumption that favorable market returns will eventually arrive is emotionally overwhelming and dangerous. The insurance side is clearly more concerned with the implications of market risk than those favoring investments, believing that even with a low probability of portfolio depletion, a retiree gets only one opportunity for a successful retirement. At the very least, they say, essential income needs should not be subject to the whims of the market. The safety-first school views investment-only solutions as undesirable because the retiree retains all the longevity and market risks, which an insurance company is in a better position to manage.

But retirement income planning is not an *either/or* proposition. We must step away from the notion that either investments or insurance alone will best serve retirees. Each tool has its own advantages and disadvantages. An entire literature on "product allocation" has arisen, showing how a more efficient set of retirement outcomes can be obtained by combining investments with insurance.

The advantages and disadvantages of investments in retirement

With investment solutions, a more comfortable lifestyle may be maintained if you are willing to invest aggressively in the hope of subsequently earning higher market returns to support a higher income rate. Should decent market returns materialize and sufficiently outpace inflation, investment solutions can be sustained indefinitely. Portfolio balances are also liquid in the technical sense that they are accessible to a retiree, not locked away as part of a contractual agreement such as an annuity. Upside growth could also support a larger legacy and provide liquidity for unexpected expenses.

However, the dual impact of sequence of returns and longevity risk leave you open to the possibility of being unable to support your desired lifestyle over the full retirement period. These are risks a retiree cannot offset easily or cheaply in an investment portfolio. Investment approaches seek to reduce sequence and longevity risk by having the retiree spend conservatively. Retirees spend less to avoid depleting their portfolio through a bad sequence of returns in early retirement, and because they must be prepared to live well beyond their life expectancy. The implication is clear: should the market perform reasonably well in retirement, the retiree will significantly underspend relative to their potential and leave an unintentionally large legacy.

At the same time, longevity protection (the risk of outliving savings) is not guaranteed with investments, and sufficient assets may not be available to support a long life or legacy. A "reverse legacy" could result if the portfolio is so depleted that the retiree must rely on others (often adult children) for support. This is particularly important in light of the ongoing improvements in mortality. On the whole, retirees of today will live longer and have to support longer retirements than their predecessors. For healthy individuals in their sixties, we are approaching the point where forty years must replace thirty years as a conservative planning horizon.

Retirees experience reduced risk capacity as they enter retirement. Their reduced flexibility to earn income leaves them more vulnerable to forced lifestyle reductions resulting from the whims of the market. A probability-based strategy could backfire.

Investment assets may also be less liquid than they appear. Though they are technically liquid, a retiree who spends assets that were meant to cover spending needs later in life may find that those later needs can no longer be met.

Additionally, with age come declining cognitive abilities, which make it increasingly difficult to manage investment and withdrawal decisions required for a systematic withdrawal strategy. However, these concerns may be offset by allowing a trusted family member to handle your finances or working with a professional financial planner.

The advantages and disadvantages of insurance in retirement

Insurance companies pool sequence and longevity risks across a large base of retirees—much like a traditional defined-benefit pension—allowing for retirement income spending that is more closely aligned with average long-term fixed income returns and longevity. This could support a higher lifestyle than that which is feasible for someone self-managing these risks by assuming low returns and a longer time horizon.

Guarantees can also provide a peace of mind for your lifestyle that leads to a less stressful and more enjoyable retirement experience. Overly conservative retirees become so concerned with running out of money that they spend significantly less than they could. A monthly annuity payment can provide the explicit permission to spend and enjoy retirement. A dependable monthly check from an annuity can also simplify life for those with reduced cognitive skills or for surviving spouses who may be less experienced with regard to financial matters.

The primary benefit of the safety-first, insurance-based approach is longevity protection, as it provides a guaranteed income for as long as you live. It hedges longevity risk and calibrates the planning horizon to something much closer to life expectancy. Those who fall short of life expectancy subsidize the income payments for those who outlive it (known as "mortality credits"). Both groups enjoy higher spending because they have pooled the longevity risk and do not have to plan based on an overly conservative time horizon. This higher income also provides flexibility to spend less than possible and maintain more reserves to manage inflation risk.

A death benefit can be created with life insurance to provide a specific legacy amount. Additionally, an income annuity dedicates assets specifically toward the provision of income, allowing other assets to be earmarked specifically for growth. This can allow for a larger legacy, especially when the retiree enjoys a long life and more of their income is supported by the annuity's mortality credits.

But many retirees may be significantly underfunded and may not be able to reach their goals even after pooling risks. Though income annuities can guarantee a lifestyle, they lack the ability to provide upside potential on their own, and inflation-protected versions are costly. In such cases, individuals may need to rely on the growth potential of their investments to achieve retirement goals and protect against inflation. Though risky, some retirees may tolerate those disadvantages and conclude that the loss of upside potential is not worth the sacrifice.

Liquidity could also be a problem with insurance solutions when unexpected expenses arise. While some annuity products offer liquidity, there is generally a high cost for this flexibility. Efforts to gain liquidity can undermine the true advantages of annuitization. Partial annuitization helps free up other assets on the balance sheet from having to support spending needs, and this combination can work to provide a greater amount of true liquidity. As for a legacy, though the death benefit in an insurance contract may grow over time, it is unlikely to keep pace with inflation. Also, income annuities do not offer legacy benefits without adding additional riders, which reduce the power of mortality credits.

Two Philosophies for Retirement Income Planning

Within the world of retirement income planning, the siloed nature of financial services between investments and insurance leads to two opposing philosophies about how to build a retirement plan. There is an old saying that if the only tool you have is a hammer, then everything starts to look like a nail. This tendency is alive as those on the investments side tend to view an investment portfolio as a solution for any problem, while those on the insurance side tend to view insurance products as the answer for any financial question.

While we have just reviewed the general benefits and disadvantages of the general categories of investments and insurance, it is worthwhile to dig deeper into how the two schools distinctly approach the retirement income challenge in an effort to bridge the gap between these two philosophies. Ultimately, we can integrate both philosophies into a comprehensive strategy that can promote more efficient overall retirement income planning and support more income and legacy.

As I said above, I distinguish the opposing schools as either *probability-based* (investments) or *safety-first* (insurance). Understanding the distinctions and thought processes of both schools is important; discussions about retirement income planning can become quite confusing. Each individual investor must ultimately identify which school can best support both their financial and psychological needs for retirement.

Indeed, advocates of the two schools view retirement income planning differently. They provide opposite answers for basic questions such as:

- Can people effectively prioritize among different financial goals in retirement?

- What is the best way to invest financial assets for retirement income?

- Is there a sustainable spending rate from a portfolio of volatile assets?

- What role do income annuities play in a retirement income strategy?

As a basic introduction to these schools, a simple litmus test can be applied. Monte Carlo simulations are often used in financial planning contexts to gain a better understanding about the viability of a financial plan in the face of market and longevity risks. Suppose a Monte Carlo simulation identifies a retirement plan's chance of success as 90%. Both sides of the debate might accept this as the correct calculation from the software, but they will have dramatically different interpretations of what to do with this number.

For probability-based thinkers, a 90% chance is a more than reasonable starting point and the retiree can proceed with the plan. It has a high likelihood of success and that's enough for them. If future updates determine that the plan might be on course toward failure, a few changes, such as a small reduction in spending, should be sufficient to get the plan back on track.

Those identifying with the safety-first school, however, will not be comfortable with this level of risk, focusing instead on the 10% chance of failure. They make a distinction between essential expenses and discretionary expenses and seek a solution that practically eliminates the possibility of failure for meeting essential expenses. Jeopardizing success, they say, is only reasonable for discretionary expenses.

Financial service professionals and retirees should understand which school they most identify with and to what extent their own thinking might incorporate views from each school. Consumers of the financial services profession must understand whether they and their advisor are speaking the same language. Advisors able to communicate effectively from both sides will be more likely to deliver successful retirement income outcomes.

The probability-based school of thought

Of the two approaches, the probability-based school of thought is probably the more familiar to the public and financial professionals. Its roots grow from research completed by California-based financial planner William Bengen in the 1990s. Bengen sought to determine the safe withdrawal rate from a financial portfolio over a long retirement. Though the term "safe withdrawal rate" uses the word "safe," it is not part of the safety-first approach. The probability-based school uses "safe" in a historical context. The probability-based approach is more closely associated with the traditional concepts of wealth accumulation and investment management.

Probability-based models tend to focus on this concept of safe withdrawal rates, a concept which is rather foreign to the safety-first school of thought. Safe withdrawal rates are about systematic withdrawals from a volatile portfolio. The question is: how much can retirees withdraw from their savings, which are invested in a diversified portfolio, while still maintaining sufficient confidence that they can safely continue spending without running out of wealth?

In the early 1990s, William Bengen read misguided claims in the popular press that average portfolio returns could guide the calculation of sustainable retirement withdrawal rates. If stocks average 7% after inflation, then plugging a 7% return into a spreadsheet suggests that retirees could withdraw 7% each year without ever dipping into their principal. Bengen recognized the naivety of ignoring the real-world volatility experienced around that 7% return, and he sought to determine what would have worked historically for hypothetical retirees at different points. He used data extending back to 1926 for U.S. financial markets for his research, which introduced the concept of "sequence of returns risk" to the financial planning profession.

The problem he set up is simple: a new retiree makes plans for withdrawing some inflation-adjusted amount from their savings at the end of each year for a thirty-year retirement period. For a sixty-five-year old, this leads to a maximum planning age of ninety-five, which Bengen felt was reasonably conservative. What is the highest withdrawal amount as a percentage of retirement date assets that, with inflation adjustments, will be sustainable for the full thirty years? He looked at rolling thirty-year periods from history (1926 to 1955, 1927 to 1956, etc.). He found that with a 50/50 asset allocation to stocks and bonds (the S&P 500 and intermediate term government bonds), the worst-case scenario experienced in U.S. history was for a hypothetical 1966 retiree who could have withdrawn 4.15% at most. Thus was born what is known as the "4% rule."

Bengen's work pointed out that sequence of returns risk will reduce safe sustainable withdrawal rates below what is implied by the average portfolio return. Its popularity has coalesced into what we are calling the probability-based approach.

Next, we'll discuss probability-based answers to some basic retirement income planning questions.

How are goals prioritized?

The idea of using a safe withdrawal rate, as implied by the 4% rule, is that people don't retire until they have accumulated a sufficient level of assets that can meet their entire lifestyle goal by spending from their portfolio at the determined safe withdrawal rate. For instance, if someone seeks to spend $40,000 per year from their portfolio and is comfortable with spending at an initial 4% rate from assets, then the wealth accumulation target to allow retirement to commence is:

Wealth = Spending/Withdrawal Rate = 40,000/0.04 = $1,000,000

According to probability-based advocates, people identify lifestyle spending needs that must be met to fulfill the standard of living they have in mind for retirement. If they are unable to meet these lifestyle spending goals, they will view their retirement as a failure. Thus, the emphasis is on minimizing the probability of failure (or, conversely, maximizing the probability of success) for the overall lifestyle goal without concern for the potential magnitude of those failures when they happen. If retirees are generally more sensitive to the probability of meeting their goals than to the magnitude of their shortfall, then it hardly matters if a retiree can spend only one-quarter or one-half less than their goal, because their lifestyle is severely diminished either way.

As suggested by the naming of the probability-based school, the objective is to develop a plan that will maximize the probability of success for meeting the overall lifestyle goal. For aggressive goals, an aggressive asset allocation may maximize success with the hope that an outsized return premium for stocks can be earned above bonds. Financial planners such as Michael Kitces and Jonathan Guyton argue that it is difficult for people to differentiate between essential needs and discretionary expenses, and that real people are not as blasé about meeting their "wants" (as opposed to needs) as safety-first advocates assume.

What is the investment approach?

The probability-based approach is based closely on the concepts of

maximizing risk-adjusted returns from the perspective of the total portfolio. Asset allocation during retirement is generally defined in the same way during the accumulation phase—using Modern Portfolio Theory (MPT) to identify a portfolio on the efficient frontier in terms of single period tradeoffs between risk and return. Different volatile asset classes that are not perfectly correlated are combined to create portfolios with lower volatility. The efficient frontier identifies the asset allocation combinations with the highest probability-weighted arithmetic average return (often called "expected return" in finance literature) for an acceptable level of year-by-year volatility (often called "risk"). This is an assets-only analysis, and the investor's spending needs are not part of the decision calculus for determining asset allocation. In addition, inputs for the efficient frontier are generally estimated from historical data. With MPT, investors aim to maximize wealth by seeking the highest possible returns given their capacity and tolerance for risk over a specific time horizon.

For retirement planning, spending and asset allocation recommendations are based on historical or Monte Carlo simulations of failure rates in order to mitigate the risk of wealth depletion inherent in drawing down a portfolio of volatile assets. The failure rate is the probability that wealth is depleted before death or before the end of the fixed time horizon, which stands in for a maximum feasible lifespan. Asset allocation decisions are generally guided by what can minimize the failure rate in retirement. Advocates of the probability-based approach take this as license to use more aggressive asset allocations than seen elsewhere (such as the rule of thumb that bond allocation should be equal to one's age).

Advice from Bengen and subsequent studies is to have a stock allocation between 50 and 75%, but as close as possible to the higher end. Probability-based advocates are generally more optimistic about the long-run potential of stocks to outperform bonds and provide positive real returns, so investors are generally advised to take on as much risk as they can tolerate in order to minimize the probability of failure.

Probability advocates generally see little value in income annuities. Income annuities have no upside potential, a cost these advocates view as too high regardless of the safety the income annuity provides. Especially with today's low interest rates, building a lifetime floor in such a way can be seen as unnecessarily expensive. Income annuities may protect a person from destitution, but, probability-based advocates argue, they could also lock out the ability to enjoy the higher quality of life people desire for their retirement.

Most retirees will not have saved enough to safely immunize their entire lifestyle spending goals through only bond ladders and income annuities while still maintaining sufficient remaining wealth to create a liquid contingency fund for unexpected expenses. If a retiree's desired withdrawal rate is above what can be generated with the bond yield curve, a bond portfolio will not be able to meet their spending goals. Bonds would actually become a drag on the portfolio as they offer no chance at the types of returns needed to fund their desired lifestyle. It is the same if the spending goal exceeds what can be obtained with an income annuity. Equity exposure moves retirees away from the guarantee that their plan will work, but it might provide the only opportunity for them to meet all of their aspirations. This aspect of probability maximization through a diversified portfolio is why we refer to this school of thought as "probability-based."

What is the safe withdrawal rate from a diversified portfolio of volatile assets?

Users of safe withdrawal rates generally treat 4% as a reasonably safe worst-case sustainable withdrawal rate for a thirty-year retirement period, although they acknowledge that a new worst-case scenario could force that number lower. Bengen now speaks regularly about 4.5% as the safe withdrawal rate, a result of also including small-capitalization stocks into the portfolio mix. He is confident that U.S. history provides a good guide about worst-case scenarios, since his analysis period includes the Great Depression, a world war, and the stagnation of the 1970s.

If people can meet lifestyle goals using a safe withdrawal rate determined from history, they can be reasonably confident about their retirement, too. Also, in all but this worst-case scenario—so the argument goes—retirees will enjoy further upside as the portfolio grows when using a conservative withdrawal rate.

Regarding upside, Kitces and Bengen both reference—as a statement of confidence in safe withdrawal rates—the fact that in 96% of the U.S. historical simulations, the value of assets remaining after thirty years was higher than the retirement date amount (although this is not adjusted for inflation). Ultimately, the idea is to retire when you can meet your spending goals from your portfolio using what you consider to be a safe withdrawal rate.

The safety-first school of thought

The safety-first school of thought was originally derived from academic models of how people allocate their resources over a lifetime to maximize lifetime satisfaction. Academics have studied these models since the 1920s to figure out how rational people make optimal decisions. In the retirement context, the question to be answered is how to get the most lifetime satisfaction from limited financial resources. It is the basic fundamental question of economics: How do you optimize in the face of scarcity? In more recent history, Nobel Prize winners such as Paul Samuelson, Robert Merton, Franco Modigliani, and William Sharpe have explored these models.

Safety-first comes from a more academic foundation, so it is often described with mathematical equations in academic journals. As a result, it has been slow to enter the public consciousness. The safety-first approach is probably best associated with Professor Zvi Bodie from Boston University, whose popular books such as *Worry Free Investing* and *Risk Less and Prosper* have brought these ideas alive to the public. Michael Zwecher's *Retirement Portfolios* is also an excellent resource written for financial professionals about this school of thought.

How are goals prioritized?

Advocates of the safety-first approach view prioritization of retirement goals as an essential component of developing a good retirement income strategy. The investment strategy aims to match the risk characteristics of assets and goals, so prioritization is a must.

Prioritizing goals has its academic origins in the idea of utility maximization. As people spend more, they experience diminishing marginal value with each additional dollar spent. The spending required to satisfy basic needs provides much more value and satisfaction to someone than the additional spending on luxuries after basic needs are met. Retirees should plan to smooth spending over time to avoid overspending on luxuries in one year and being unable to afford essentials later.

In developing Modern Retirement Theory, financial planner Jason Branning and academic M. Ray Grubbs created a funding priority for retiree liabilities. Essential needs are the top priority, then a contingency fund, funds for discretionary expenses, and a legacy fund. They illustrate these funding priorities with a pyramid. Building a retirement strategy requires working from the bottom to properly fund each goal before moving up to the next. There is no consideration of discretionary expenses or providing a legacy until a secure funding source for essential needs and contingencies is in place.

What is the investment approach?

Traditionally, investing in the accumulation phase has built on the tools of Modern Portfolio Theory (MPT) and portfolio diversification to find a suitable balance between investment returns and the volatility of those returns. Investors seek strategies that will support the highest expected wealth, subject to the investor's tolerance and capacity to endure downward fluctuations in the portfolio value. But, this was never the complete story. In 1991, Nobel laureate and MPT founder Harry Markowitz wrote in the first issue of *Financial Services Review* about how MPT was never meant to apply to the investment problems of a household. Rather, it was for large institutions with indefinite lifespans and no specific spending objectives for the portfolio. This should have been a eureka moment for the entire retirement income industry, but MPT is still misapplied today.

People have finite lifespans. The purpose of saving and investing is to fund spending during retirement. MPT does not address this more complicated issue. The alternative is asset-liability matching, which focuses more holistically at the household level and also emphasizes hedging and insurance. In simple terms, hedging means holding individual bonds to maturity, and insurance means using income annuities as a solution for longevity and market risk.

With asset-liability matching, investors are not trying to maximize their year-to-year returns on a risk-adjusted basis, nor are they trying to beat an investing benchmark. The goal is to have cash flows available to meet spending needs as required, and investments are chosen in such a way that meets those needs. Assets are matched to goals so that the risk and cash flow characteristics are comparable. For essential spending, Modern Retirement Theory argues that funding must be with assets meeting the criteria of being "secure, stable, and sustainable." Funding options can include defined-benefit pensions, bond ladders, and income annuities. In this regard, another important aspect of the investment approach for the safety-first school is that investing decisions are made in the context of the entire household balance sheet. This moves beyond looking only at the financial portfolio to consider also the role of human and social capital. Examples of human and social capital include the ability to work part-time, pensions, the social safety net, and so on.

An important point is that volatile assets are seen as inappropriate for basic needs and the contingency fund. Stated again, the objective of investing in retirement is not to maximize risk-adjusted returns, but first to ensure that basics will be covered in any market environment and then to invest for additional upside. Volatile (and hopefully, but not necessarily, higher returning) assets are suitable for discretionary expenses and legacy, in which there is some flexibility about whether the spending can be achieved.

Asset allocation, therefore, is an output of the analysis, as the entire household balance sheet is used and assets are allocated to match appropriately with the household's liabilities. Asset-liability matching removes the probability-based concept of safe withdrawal rates from the analysis, since it rejects relying on a diversified portfolio for the entire lifestyle goal.

The idea is to first build a floor of very low-risk guaranteed income sources to serve your basic spending needs in retirement. The guaranteed income floor is built with Social Security and any other defined-benefit pensions, and through the use of your financial assets to do things such as building a ladder of TIPS or purchasing an income annuity. Not all of these income sources are inflation adjusted, and you need to make sure the floor is sufficiently protected from inflation, but this is the basic idea.

Once there is a sufficient floor in place, you can focus on upside potential. With any remaining assets, you can invest and spend as you wish. Since this extra spending (such as for nice restaurants, extra vacations, etc.) is discretionary, it won't be the end of the world if you must reduce spending at some point. You still have your guaranteed income floor in place to meet your basic needs no matter what happens. With this sort of approach, withdrawal rates hardly matter.

What is the safe withdrawal rate from a diversified portfolio of volatile assets?

The general view of safety-first advocates is that there is no such thing as a safe withdrawal rate from a volatile portfolio. A truly safe withdrawal rate is unknown and unknowable. Retirees only receive one opportunity to obtain sustainable cash flows from their savings and must develop a strategy that will meet basic needs no matter the length of life or the sequence of post-retirement market returns and inflation. Retirees have little leeway for error, as returning to the labor force might not be a realistic option. Volatile assets like stocks are not appropriate when seeking to meet basic retirement living expenses. Just because a strategy did not fail over a historical period does not ensure it will always succeed in the future.

The objective for retirement is first to build a safe and secure income floor for the entire retirement planning horizon, and only after that should you include more volatile assets that provide greater upside potential and accompanying risk. In terms of this floor for essentials and contingencies, pensions, bond ladders, and income annuities should take the lead. Failure should not be an option when meeting basic needs. Thus, income annuities serve as a fundamental building block for retirement income.

Income annuities are especially valuable because of their ability to provide longevity protection through the provision of mortality credits. People do not know their age of death in advance. They can learn about their remaining life expectancy, but that is just a projection of the average outcome and there is a surprisingly large distribution of actual lifespans around the average. Individual retirees cannot self-insure to protect from longevity risk, and without annuitization they are obliged to plan for a long lifespan.

The annuity provider, however, can pool longevity risk across a large group of retirees, and those who die earlier than average subsidize payments to those who live longer than average. These are mortality credits. Because the annuity provider can pool the longevity risk, they are able to make payments at a rate much closer to what would be possible when planning for remaining life expectancy. A retiree seeking to *self-annuitize* must assume a time horizon extending well beyond life expectancy (such as thirty years with the 4% rule), to better hedge against the consequences of living beyond their planning age. A retiree must spend less when on the self-annuitize path.

Retirement Income Strategies

This discussion of the two schools of thought highlights that retirement income planning is a field in flux. Exhibit 1.5 highlights this matter with just a sampling of different retirement income planning techniques used in practice today. The table includes thirty-six possibilities, which I have attempted to differentiate in part by whether they have characteristics more similar to the probability-based or safety-first philosophy.

Many more strategies could be listed in the "Total Returns/Variable Spending" category, as it seems almost every financial services company is developing a retirement income strategy these days. Most of the excluded strategies would be difficult to distinguish from what is already on the list, though.

My aim is to simplify this list by narrowing down the options to some core attributes that can serve as best practices. I have studied all of these different approaches and tried to draw what is best from each to build an overall framework to guide retirement income planning.

Exhibit 1.6 Retirement Income Optimization Plan©

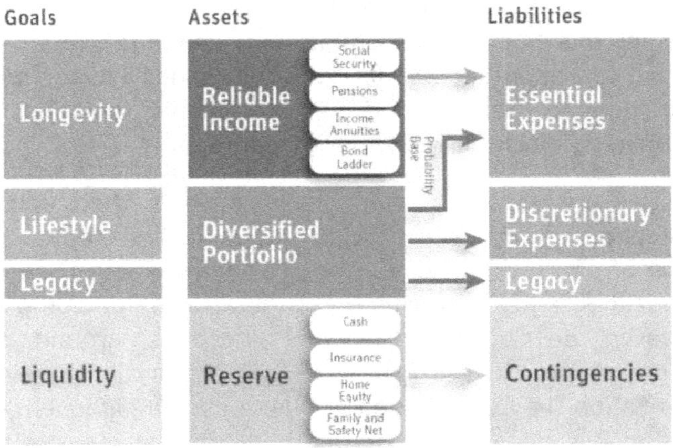

Ultimately, I believe Exhibit 1.6 provides a proper summary of how to approach the retirement income problem. This exhibit draws on attributes from the safety-first approach to consider the entire household balance sheet and to match assets and liabilities. It is most inspired by ideas found within Modern Retirement Theory, the Household Balance Sheet View, Funded Ratio Management, and Product Allocation. At the same time, this approach is not overly regimented and includes both probability-based and safety-first plans, as the relative sizes of the reliable income and diversified portfolio boxes can be adjusted to create a plan that meets the psychological needs of the individual implementing it.

In a sense, the remainder of this book will discuss different approaches for structuring home equity into this diagram. Let us begin.

Further Reading

Barrett, William P. 2011. "The Retirement Spending Solution." *Forbes* [profile on William Bengen] [Link]

Bodie, Zvi, and Michael J. Clowes. 2003. *Worry-Free Investing: A Safe Approach to Achieving Your Lifetime Financial Goals.* Upper Saddle River, New Jersey: Financial Times Prentice Hall.

Bodie, Zvi, and Rachelle Taqqu. 2012. *Risk Less and Prosper: Your Guide to Safer Investing.* Hoboken, NJ: Wiley. [Link]

Branning, Jason K., and M. Ray Grubbs. 2010. "Using a Hierarchy of Funds to Reach Client Goals." *Journal of Financial Planning* 23, 12 (December): 31-33.

Kitces, Michael. 2011. "What Happens If You Outlive Your Safe Withdrawal Rate Time Horizon?" *Nerd's Eye View* blog. [Link]

Zwecher, Michael J. 2010. *Retirement Portfolios: Theory, Construction, and Management.* Hoboken, NJ: John Wiley & Sons. [Link]

CHAPTER 2: HOUSING DECISIONS IN RETIREMENT

Should I Stay or Should I Go?

Developing a plan to meet housing needs is an important part of a retirement income strategy. A home provides an emotional anchor of daily comfort, shelter, memories, and proximity to both friends and community. It is also a major source of wealth for retirees and near-retirees. For many Americans, home equity provides a substantial part of their net worth, and it is often larger than the value of the household's investment portfolio.

Expenses related to the home (property taxes, utility bills, home maintenance, and upkeep) can add up to a significant portion of the overall household budget. The Center for Retirement Research at Boston College analyzed numbers for retired couples aged sixty-five to seventy-four in 2010 and found that housing expenses represented 30% of the typical household budget.

Joseph Coughlin, the director of the MIT Agelab, created three basic questions to identify quality of life issues for retirement:

- Who will change my light bulbs?
- How will I get an ice cream cone?
- Who will I have lunch with?

An essential part of answering these questions involves solving for the right type and location of housing. These questions illustrate how our lives will change as our bodies slow down and health issues or other aspects of aging make us less mobile. They focus on:

- whether we can continue to live in and properly maintain the same home,
- whether we have access to a community that lets us continue to enjoy basic conveniences even if we may stop driving our own cars, and
- what will happen to our social lives and opportunities to remain active as old friends also become less mobile or move away.

Will we live in communities that keep these key aspects of quality living accessible to us? For new retirees, any difficulty with answering these questions may still reside in the distant future, but the major life changes associated with retirement provide a good opportunity to reflect on the different possibilities and develop a set of contingency plans.

Ultimately, one of the greatest dangers to quality of life in retirement is the risk of becoming increasingly isolated and having only television to pass the time. On the emotional side, the housing decision may relate in large part to figuring out how to best answer Coughlin's three questions over the long term.

Because of its important connection to the emotional and financial aspects of retirement, it is worthwhile to spend time thinking about housing options and potential uses for home equity. As you grow older, the importance of living somewhere with social connections, transportation options, quality health care, and long-term care services increases. Back to the more immediate present, you need to think about where to live, how long to stay there, and whether to move later in retirement. Plenty of justifications exist for staying put or for moving early in retirement.

First, consider reasons for moving. These relate primarily to the changing emphasis of life priorities and life needs. For instance, empty-nesters may no longer require a home large enough to accommodate their entire family. Large homes require more cleaning, maneuvering, heating and cooling, and maintenance. Children may have moved to other parts of the country, and new retirees may wish to be closer to their grandchildren.

While you work and raise children, you are pretty firmly locked in place by proximity to your job and your kids' school. Upon retirement, a move to a community with a less highly rated school and no concerns for your daily commute could mean lower property taxes and increased savings for your retirement budget. Additional savings could be found by moving to a state with a more tax friendly environment for retirees. This newfound freedom can create a whole new set of options that may not have been realistic in the past. In addition, with more time to focus on hobbies and interests, moving could provide an opportunity to live closer to the types of places that can better fulfill these interests (e.g., a college town or a warmer climate).

Finally, the aging process will slowly reduce mobility, and moving can be one way to set a long-term housing plan in motion to increase your chances of aging in place and having quick access to important medical care.

That being said, most retirees will choose to stay put in retirement. In fact, evidence suggests that staying put is more common than you might believe. For instance, Richard Green and Hyojung Lee studied households using the 2006-2010 American Community Survey and found that the propensity to move peaks in an individual's twenties and then declines until about fifty, where it subsequently stays at the lowest relative levels. Older individuals are less likely to move, and the rate of people who move does not rise at typical retirement ages.

Retirees have family, community ties, and friendships they do not wish to leave behind. Many have significant memories and good feelings about their homes and wish to maintain the stability and familiarity those represent. A home can be an important part of your emotional identity, and leaving that anchor behind is not a viable option for many.

Homeowners tend to take pride in ownership and might feel trepidation about going through the whole process again. New technologies and the possibility of renovating your home can also make aging in place an easier endeavor than in the past.

Exhibit 2.1 provides a summary of considerations regarding whether to stay or move in retirement.

Exhibit 2.1 Items to Consider When Deciding to Stay or Move

- Availability of interesting leisure activities
- Diverse transportation options
- Access to quality health care
- Agreeable climate and community
- Access to family and friends
- Ability to maintain social ties
- Ability to age in place in your home
- Housing prices
- Costs of living and affordability of new location
- State income taxes
- State sales tax
- State inheritance tax
- Local property taxes and costs of municipal services
- Other state tax rules regarding retirement income sources (e.g., Social Security)

Aging in Place

Another important consideration when deciding to stay put or move is whether a foundation exists to comfortably support aging in place. This concept refers to the growing industry around helping the aging population remain in their homes despite functional or cognitive impairments. Individuals benefit from the ability to maintain the familiarity and comfort of their own homes, and proper planning could help delay the need to move toward more institutional settings later in retirement. The following table provides a list of issues to consider when searching for a home and community that can support aging in place.

Merrill Lynch and AgeWave conducted a survey of retirees aged 50 and older and found that 85% viewed their own home as the top preference for receiving long-term care. Home care is often the more desirable and less expensive option. With sufficient planning, home care can be extended. Government agencies have expressed support for the idea and have promoted the concept, as aging in place often requires less contribution from government programs like Medicaid than nursing homes or assisted-living facilities.

Exhibit 2.2 Conditions to Facilitate Aging In Place

Home Characteristics and Renovations (Universal Design Features)

- Walk in showers and other bathroom safety features such as grab bars
- Single floor living that doesn't require stairs (kitchen, bathing facility, and bedroom all on one floor), or an elevator allowing access to other floors
- Wheelchair accessibility: ramps to the home, wide doors and hallways that can fit a wheelchair, at least one wheelchair-accessible entrance to the home
- Levers for door handles and faucets rather than a twisting knob
- Good lighting in case sight is diminished
- Accessible cabinets and closets as well as lowered counters to allow for cooking while sitting
- Softened flooring to help cushion any falls, but no rugs or other floor items that could create a tripping hazard
- Accessible electric controls and switches that are not too high off the ground
- New technologies to monitor health status and medicine use

Community Infrastructure

- Trusted support for home maintenance activities such as lawn care, snow removal, and home maintenance
- Overall degree of neighborhood safety
- Availability of someone (family or friend) who can provide occasional checks and help you avoid isolation
- Availability of cleaning and food delivery services (including groceries)
- Availability of transportation options outside of using your own car, such as public transportation, taxis or services like Uber, or volunteer services from non-profit organizations
- Access to a social network and enjoyable social activities
- Access to quality health care and long term care

Aging in place requires planning, and there are several potential paths. If you are staying put, home renovations can make it livable even with physical or cognitive impairments. If you are moving, the focus can shift to finding a new home with the necessary renovations already in place and to finding a community where many types of care are readily accessible. This sort of move could be to a single-home, condo/apartment, community specifically designed for fifty-five+ or sixty-two+ living, or to an Assisted Living Facility (ALF) or Continuing Care Retirement Community (CCRC).

Downsizing Your Home

One method for freeing home equity for other uses is to downsize your home. Downsizing doesn't necessarily mean moving to a physically smaller home. It could also mean moving to a similar-sized home with a smaller price tag.

The arithmetic of converting home equity through downsizing is fairly basic. If you've paid off the mortgage on a $300,000 home, and then sell it and move into a $200,000 home, $100,000 of home equity has been freed up for other uses.

Another possibility is simply selling your home and renting an apartment. Renting frees up home equity and provides the flexibility to make more frequent moves before settling down.

When analyzing the decision to rent or buy, you'll need to consider factors such as:

• the loss of build-up in home equity and its subsequent growth (or loss),

• savings on property taxes and other types of home maintenance, and

• the ongoing expense for rent that will add up significantly over time.

When downsizing, you might consider moving to an active community for adults, which could be less expensive and provide organized activities and social support. These types of communities generally do not provide health care or assisted living options. Continuing Care Retirement Communities (CCRCs) can be an option if you want to make a move that will also cover potential long-term care needs in the future without requiring a big move later in life. There are differences in home ownership with these options, as CCRCs generally provide a right to access housing for life (up through nursing care) rather than tangible equity in a home.

If you are looking to downsize for financial reasons, you may wish to first consider whether there are opportunities through local governments for property tax deferral or other possibilities. Other options include renting out a portion of your existing home or opening a reverse mortgage (more on this shortly).

An important caveat about the downsizing option is that it can be dangerous to assume downsizing will be part of your retirement income plan. The same study of retirees conducted by Merrill Lynch and AgeWave also found what they refer to as a "Downsize Surprise," where many retirees who planned to downsize ended up not wanting to do so once they retired.

The survey—composed of retirees fifty and older—revealed that 37% have moved in retirement, another 27% have not moved but anticipate moving at some point, and 36% of retirees do not anticipate moving in retirement. For those not planning to move, the top reason provided was "I love my home."

The highest ranking reasons for moving included wanting to be closer to family and reducing home expenses. For those who had moved since retirement, 51% moved to a smaller home, 19% to a same-sized home, and 30% to a larger home. For those who chose to upsize, the most important reason given was to have more space for family members (including grandchildren) to visit. The AgeWave study makes clear that downsizing is not the only moving option for retirees, and it should not be viewed as a given.

Further Reading

Center for Retirement Research at Boston College. 2014. *Using Your House for Income in Retirement.* [Link]

Coughlin, Joseph F. 2013. "3 Questions Predict Future Quality of Life.

MarketWatch RetireMentors Series (April 17). [Link]

Green, Richard. 2013. "Who Moves? Not Old People." *Forbes* (July 23). [Link]

Merrill Lynch and Age Wave. 2015. "Home in Retirement: More Freedom, New Choices." [Link]

CHAPTER 3: REVERSE MORTGAGE BACKGROUND AND HISTORY

If, after considering other housing options, you have decided to remain in an eligible home or to move into a new eligible home, you may want to consider a Home Equity Conversion Mortgage (HECM - commonly pronounced "heck-um")—more commonly known as a "reverse mortgage"— as a source of retirement spending. The vast majority of reverse mortgages in the United States are HECM reverse mortgages, which are regulated and insured through the federal government by the Department of Housing and Urban Development (HUD) and the Federal Housing Authority (FHA). Other options outside of the federal program pop up occasionally, like jumbo reverse mortgages for those seeking amounts that exceed federal limits. The HECM program includes both fixed-and variable-rate loans, though fixed-rate loans only allow proceeds to be taken as an initial lump sum, with no subsequent access to a line of credit. We will not concern ourselves with fixed-rate or non-HECM loans here. Instead, we will focus only on variable-rate HECM options.

In the past, any discussion of reverse mortgages as a retirement income tool typically focused on real or perceived negatives related to traditionally high costs and potentially inappropriate uses of these funds. These conversations often include misguided ideas about the homeowner losing the title to their home and hyperbole about the "American Dream" becoming the "American Nightmare." Reverse mortgages are portrayed as a desperate last resort.

However, developments of the past decade have made reverse mortgages harder to dismiss outright. Especially, since 2013, the federal government has been refining regulations for its HECM program in order to:

• improve the sustainability of the underlying mortgage insurance fund,

• better protect eligible non-borrowing spouses, and

• ensure borrowers have sufficient financial resources to continue paying their property taxes, homeowner's insurance, and home maintenance expenses.

The thrust of these changes has been to ensure reverse mortgages are used responsibly as part of an overall retirement income strategy, rather than to fritter away assets.

On the academic side, several recent research articles have demonstrated how responsible use of a reverse mortgage can enhance an overall retirement income plan. Importantly, this research incorporates realistic costs for reverse mortgages, both in relation to their initial upfront costs and the ongoing growth of any outstanding loan balance. Quantified benefits are understood to exist only after netting out the costs associated with reverse mortgages. This research is the focus of chapter six.

In short, well-handled reverse mortgages have suffered from the bad press surrounding irresponsible reverse mortgages for too long. Reverse mortgages give responsible retirees the option to create liquidity for an otherwise illiquid asset, which can, in turn, potentially support a more efficient retirement income strategy (more spending and/or more legacy). Liquidity is created by allowing homeowners to borrow against the value of the home with the flexibility to defer repayment until they have permanently left the home.

The media has been picking up on these developments as of late, and coverage is improving. Here is a short list of recent articles in the popular press which have spoken positively about reverse mortgages:

Dan Kadlec, "Retirees' biggest asset may be hiding in plain sight." *Time,* February 15, 2016, p. 22.

Andrea Coombes, "How to Retire in a Bear Market." *Wall Street* Journal, March 7, 2016, p. R1.

Robert Powell, "New Math on Reverse Mortgages." *Wall Street Journal,* March 21, 2016, p. R4.

Patricia Mertz Esswein, "Reverse Mortgages Get a Makeover." Kiplinger's Personal Finance, *April 2016, p. 39-40.*

But the trend of positive coverage is still a new phenomenon, and with so much pre-existing bias, it can be hard to view reverse mortgages objectively without a clear understanding of how the benefits exceed the costs. To understand their role, it is worth stepping back to clarify the retirement income problems we seek to solve (as outlined in chapter one).

Retirees must support a series of expenses—overall lifestyle spending goals, unexpected contingencies, legacy goals—to enjoy a successful retirement. Suppose retirees only have two assets—beyond Social Security and any pensions—to meet their spending obligations: an investment portfolio and home equity. The task is to link these assets to spending obligations efficiently while also mitigating retirement risks like longevity, market volatility, and spending surprises that can impact the plan.

The fundamental question is this: How can these two assets work to meet spending goals while simultaneously preserving remaining assets to cover contingencies and support a legacy? Spending from either asset today means less for future spending and legacy. For the portfolio, spending reduces the remaining asset balance and sacrifices subsequent growth on those investments. Likewise, spending a portion of home equity surrenders future legacy through the increase and subsequent growth of the loan balance. Both effects work in the same way, so the question is how to best coordinate the use of these two assets to meet the spending goal and still preserve as much legacy as possible.

When a household has an investment portfolio and home equity, the "default" strategy tends to value spending down investment assets first and preserving home equity as long as possible, with the goal of supporting a legacy through a debt-free home. A reverse mortgage is viewed as an option, but it's only a last resort once the investment portfolio has been depleted and vital spending needs are threatened.

The research of the last few years has generally found this conventional wisdom constraining and counterproductive. Initiating the reverse mortgage earlier and coordinating spending from home equity throughout retirement can help meet spending goals while also providing a larger legacy. That is the nature of retirement income efficiency: using assets in a way that allows for more spending and/or more legacy.

Legacy wealth is the combined value of any remaining financial assets plus any remaining home equity after repaying the reverse mortgage. Money is fungible and the specific ratio of financial assets and remaining home equity is not important. In the final analysis, only the sum of these two components matters.

For heirs wishing to keep the home, a larger legacy offers an extra bonus of additional financial assets after the loan balance has been repaid. The home is *not* lost.

While taking money from the reverse mortgage reduces the home equity component, it does not necessarily reduce the overall net worth or legacy value of assets. Wanting to specifically preserve the home may be a psychological constraint, which leads to a less efficient retirement. As Tom Davison of ToolsforRetirementPlanning.com has described the matter to me in our discussions, a reverse mortgage allows a retiree to gift the value of the house rather than the house itself. Should the heir wish to keep the house, the value of the house they have received as an inheritance can be redeployed for this purpose.

The Underlying Mechanisms of How Reverse Mortgages Can Help

Two benefits give opening a reverse mortgage earlier in retirement the potential to improve retirement efficiencies in spite of loan costs. First, coordinating withdrawals from a reverse mortgage reduces strain on portfolio withdrawals, which helps manage sequence of returns risk. Investment volatility is amplified by sequence of returns risk and can be more harmful to retirees who are withdrawing from, rather than contributing to their portfolio. Reverse mortgages sidestep this sequence risk by providing an alternative source of spending after market declines.

The second potential benefit of opening the reverse mortgage early—especially when interest rates are low—is that the principal limit that can be borrowed from will continue to grow throughout retirement. Reverse mortgages are non-recourse loans, meaning that even if the loan balance is greater than the subsequent home value, the borrower does not have to repay more than their home is worth. Sufficiently long retirements carry a reasonable possibility that the available credit may eventually exceed the value of the home. In these cases, mortgage insurance premiums paid to the government are used to make sure the lender does not experience a loss. In addition, the borrower and/or estate will not be on the hook for repaying more than the value of the home when the loan becomes due. This line of credit growth is one of the most important and confusing aspects of reverse mortgages. I will return to line of credit growth for a deeper explanation later.

As the government continues to strengthen the rules and regulations for reverse mortgages and new research continues to pave the way with an agnostic view of their role, reverse mortgages may become much more common in the coming years. Many Americans rely on home equity and Social Security as the two primary available retirement assets.

As Dr. Sandra Timmerman, gerontologist and visiting professor at The American College, said, "The transition to retirement is a wake-up call for many middle-income Baby Boomers who haven't saved enough money to last a lifetime and want to age in place. With their homes as a major untapped financial resource, the smart use of reverse mortgages will be their saving grace."

Addressing the Bad Reputation of Reverse Mortgages

Before discussing how reverse mortgages can fit into your retirement income plan, it is worthwhile to first consider in greater detail the bad reputation reverse mortgages have developed. Some aspects of that bad reputation are based on misunderstandings, some were once true but have since been mitigated, and some may still remain.

When considering a reverse mortgage, it is important to be responsible with the strategy and not give in to the temptation to treat the reverse mortgage as a windfall and spend it quickly. This point cannot be overemphasized enough, as the natural tendency may be to spend assets as soon as they become liquid. Responsible retirees have little to worry about, but if you lack sufficient self-control, reverse mortgages should be handled carefully.

Irresponsible borrowers who quickly deplete their assets and suffer later in retirement are part of the reason reverse mortgages developed their bad reputation. Recent government changes have been designed to encourage more responsible use, but in many cases, the compensation for loan officers originating these mortgages still may be linked to the initial borrowing amount. Loan officers may suggest taking more out sooner as a result. Consequently, borrowers should seek a loan originator who is not compensated based on the initial lump sum taken from the loan, unless they are also working with a trusted financial planner who can help manage this process.

Troubles regarding reverse mortgages are summarized in Exhibit 3.1. Some of the troubles relate to misunderstandings, such as the idea that the lender receives the title to the home, or simple miscommunication among family members about future inheritances.

Other troubles relate to problems that have since been corrected by new HUD regulations. Some of these problems include concerns about withdrawing too much too soon, the potential problems confronting non-borrowing spouses, and foreclosures for desperate borrowers who could not keep up with their property taxes, homeowner's insurance, and home maintenance requirements.

Other problems have been addressed by the government, though these issues are not necessarily fully resolved. For many lenders, a notable cost is still involved in initiating a reverse mortgage, though these upfront costs have been reduced in recent years and some lenders can now offer minimal upfront costs. I also have concerns about whether the mortgage insurance premiums collected by the government will be sufficient to cover the non-recourse aspects of the reverse mortgage, especially if some of the strategies I discuss grow in popularity.

Exhibit 3.1 Addressing the Bad Reputation of Reverse Mortgages

Reasons Reverse Mortgages Have Bad Reputations	Further Discussion
Use Reverse Mortgage Too Quickly for Questionable Expenses	
In the past, retirees have opened a reverse mortgage in order to immediately spend the full amount of available credit—perhaps either to overindulge irresponsibly in unnecessary discretionary expenses or to finance shady or even fraudulent investment or insurance products. This jeopardized the role of home equity as a contingency asset for the household.	HUD requires a counseling session and has enacted new rules to discourage taking too much too soon from the available line of credit. As of 2015, the mortgage insurance premium increased from 0.5% to 2.5% of the home value if more than 60% of the available proceeds are withdrawn in the first calendar year. Also, more than 60% of the available credit can be spent in the first year only for particular qualified expenses such as to pay off an existing mortgage or to use the HECM for Purchase program.
Family Misunderstandings	
The media has reported on adult children who are surprised to find they will not inherit the house after their parents passed because their parents used a reverse mortgage.	Such media reports are typically based on misunderstandings on the part of angry children. Articles focus on only one aspect of inheritance (the home), and do not consider how to best meet the retirement spending needs of parents. Children can pay the loan balance and keep the home, and recent research clarifies (see chapter six) that strategic use of a reverse mortgage to cover a fixed retirement spending need is actually more likely to increase the overall amount of legacy wealth available to children at the end. One must also consider whether the parents' assets were best used to meet their own spending goals or to be provided as a legacy for their children.
Non-Borrowing Spouses	
In the past, younger spouses were taken off the home title to allow a reverse mortgage to proceed, only to be surprised when the borrower died and the non-borrowing spouse either had to repay the loan or leave the home.	As of 2015, new protections are in place for these non-borrowing spouses. They can remain on the home title and stay in the home even after the borrowing spouse has passed away. Though non-borrowing spouses cannot borrow more from the line of credit, they are now able to remain in the home, and lending limits will be based on their age to help protect the insurance fund. Eligible non-borrowing spouses no longer have to worry about loan repayment until they leave the home.
Reasons Reverse Mortgages Have Bad Reputations	**Further Discussion**
Taxpayer Risk	
People may worry about taxpayers being on the hook if the mortgage insurance fund is overburdened by the non-recourse aspects of the loans.	Reduced housing prices in the 2000s created problems that would be addressed with the Reverse Mortgage Stabilization Act of 2013, which sought to help make sure insurance premiums and lending limits were sufficient to keep the insurance self-sustaining. Nonetheless, this situation may not be fully resolved at the present, especially when interest rates are currently low and may rise in the future.
Stigma About Using Debt	
Psychologically, individuals may be challenged by the idea of using a debt instrument in retirement after having spent their careers working to reduce their debt.	This is a psychological constraint. If you think about your investment portfolio and home equity as assets, then meeting spending goals requires spending from assets somewhere on the household balance sheet. In this regard, spending from home equity would not be framed as accumulating debt any more than spending from investment assets. A reverse mortgage creates liquidity for an otherwise illiquid asset.

Reasons Reverse Mortgages Have Bad Reputations	Further Discussion
Home Title	
Many people hold the common misconception that the lender receives the title to the home as part of a reverse mortgage.	This enduring myth about the HECM program is simply untrue.
Desperate Borrowers	
Reverse mortgages were taken out by those who were unable to keep up with their property taxes, homeowner's insurance premiums, and home upkeep. This could result in a default that triggers foreclosure.	As of 2015, a financial assessment is required to ensure that the borrower has the capacity to make these payments. If other resources are not available, set-asides will be carved out of the line of credit to support these payments. These do not become part of the loan balance until they are spent, but they do otherwise limit the amount you can borrow from the line of credit. Nonetheless, to the extent that the liquidity from the reverse mortgage leads to a behavioral issue of overspending, this is a concern for potential borrowers with limited self control.
Foreclosure	
Foreclosures for the elderly generated by the inability to meet technical requirements of the loan generated negative media coverage and a misconstrued view of the HECM program.	New safeguards have been added, but it is important to keep in mind that such retirements were not sustainable in the first place. A reverse mortgage may have still created net positive impacts for the households, as their living situation could have otherwise worsened much sooner. Reverse mortgages do not require monthly repayments, so non-payment of the loan cannot trigger foreclosure. The reverse mortgage may have helped delay what was ultimately inevitable.
High Costs	
Reverse mortgages are expensive to initiate.	In the past, the initial costs for opening reverse mortgages could be as high as 6% of the home value. These upfront costs have been reduced dramatically for competitive lenders. Nonetheless, HECM loans originated today include an unavoidable 0.5% upfront mortgage insurance premium. That adds up to $500 per $100,000 of appraised home value. Other closing costs for home appraisal, titling, and other matters similar to traditional mortgages cannot be avoided. That being said, many lenders may charge the full allowed amount for origination charges, so consumers must shop around. There are currently no easy ways to compare offers from different lenders.

A Brief History of Reverse Mortgages in the United States

Reverse mortgages have a relatively short history in the United States, beginning in a bank in Maine in 1961. The 1987 Housing and Community Development Act saw the federal government systemize reverse mortgages through the Home Equity Conversion Mortgage (HECM) program under the auspices of the U.S. Department of Housing and Urban Development (HUD).

I intend to focus only on HECM reverse mortgages, which are tightly regulated and represent the bulk of reverse mortgages. I will not be discussing programs such as those offered through local governments to provide liquidity for a more limited purpose, or proprietary reverse mortgages, which may appeal to those with homes worth more than the $625,500 FHA lending limit on home values. (A HECM can be obtained on homes worth more than $625,500, but the funds available through the reverse mortgage will be based on the lesser of the home's appraised value and $625,500.)

In recent years, HUD has frequently updated the administration of the HECM program to address various issues and ensure reverse mortgages are used responsibly. As a result, descriptions of the program can quickly become outdated, even if they are only a couple years old. While older materials may explain the concepts adequately, they might be missing key changes.

Lender standards have tightened and the number of new reverse mortgages issued has declined after peaking around 110,000 per year in 2008 and 2009. Many borrowers at the peak were financially constrained and unable to keep up with taxes, insurance, and home maintenance. Among those who borrowed, many opted to take out the full available initial credit amount as a lump sum. After spending this down quickly, they were left with no other assets, which led to a number of foreclosures. On top of that, falling home prices meant many loan balances exceeded the value of the home being used as collateral when repayment was due, which put greater pressure on the mortgage insurance fund.

Many resources on reverse mortgages describe two versions: the HECM Standard and HECM Saver. The HECM Saver was introduced in October 2010 as a contrast to HECM Standard and in response to increased foreclosures. It provided access to a smaller percentage of the home's value, substantially reducing borrowers' mortgage insurance premiums. It represented a step toward encouraging less upfront use of reverse mortgage credit, but it went largely unused by borrowers.

By September 2013, the Saver and Standard again merged into a single HECM option. The newly merged program provided an initial credit amount that was slightly larger than that of the HECM Saver but substantially less than the HECM Standard. Principal Limit Factors (more on these later) were recalculated to lower available borrowing amounts.

The government also sought to encourage deliberate, conservative use of home equity by implementing penalties and limits. If more than 60% of the initial line of credit was spent during the first year, the borrower was charged a higher upfront mortgage insurance premium on the home's appraised value (2.5% instead of 0.5%). For a $500,000 home with a $237,500 principal limit, the initial mortgage insurance premium jumps from $2,500 to $12,500 if more than $142,500 is spent from the line of credit in year one—a $10,000 incentive to lower spending. In addition, borrowing more than 60% of the principal limit is now only allowed for qualified mandatory expenses like paying down an existing mortgage or using the HECM for Purchase program.

Before September 2013, the HECM Standard mortgage had an initial

mortgage insurance premium of 2% of the home value, so the upfront costs for opening a reverse mortgage dropped significantly for those who could stay under the 60% limit after HECM Standard and Saver merged. Yet it still paled in comparison to the HECM Saver, as the new 0.5% upfront mortgage premium was considerably higher than the previous 0.01% value. So while the new rules were designed to encourage more gradual and deliberate HECM use, the costs for setting up this opportunity relative to the HECM Saver increased.

Two important additional consumer safeguards came into full effect in 2015. The first relates to new protections for non-borrowing spouses who don't meet the minimum age requirement of sixty-two. In the past, when one spouse was too young, the solution was typically to remove that spouse from the house title. This created a problem when the borrowing spouse died first and the loan balance became due. Without sufficient liquidity or the ability to refinance, the non-borrowing spouse could be forced out of the home.

HUD implemented safeguards for non-borrowing spouses in 2014 and further clarified them the following year. As of spring 2015, non-borrowing spouses now have the right to stay in the home after the borrower dies or leaves, as the loan balance no longer needs to be paid until after the non-borrowing spouse has also left the home. In order to do this, the non-borrowing spouse must have been the spouse when the loan was closed, must be named as a non-borrowing spouse, and must continue to occupy the property as a primary residence and maintain the usual taxes, insurance, and home upkeep. To be clear, while the non-borrowing spouse may stay in the home, they are not borrowers. Once the borrower has left the home, there is no further ability to spend from the line of credit, and any term or tenure payments stop. However, interest and mortgage insurance premiums continue to accrue on any outstanding loan balance. The existing rules contain an important caveat: should the borrower move to an institution such as a nursing home for at least twelve months, the loan may become due even if the non-borrowing spouse remains in the home.

The most recent versions of the principal limit factors (PLFs), published on August 4, 2014, now account for non-borrowing spouses. PLFs are now provided for ages eighteen and older to account for non-borrowing spouses who are significantly younger than the borrower. Before these changes, PLFs were only needed for ages sixty-two and older. The PLF is based on the younger of the borrower and non-borrowing spouse.

Though non-borrowing spouses cannot spend from the reverse mortgage, they may remain in the home for many more years, so initial HECM proceeds must be lowered to protect against loan balances exceeding the home's value. Aside from the expansion to account for non-borrowing spouses, the August 2014 PLFs underwent further downward revisions to limit the initial available credit amount in order to ensure mortgage insurance premiums could cover the risk of loan balances exceeding the home's value.

The other new consumer safeguard implemented in 2014 and effective in 2015 is a more detailed financial assessment for potential borrowers to ensure they will have sufficient means to pay property taxes, homeowner's insurance, maintenance and upkeep, and other homeowner's association dues. Determination that a potential borrower will struggle to meet these obligations with assets from outside home equity will not disqualify them from receiving a HECM. Life expectancy set-asides (LESAs) can now be carved out of the line of credit to cover these expenses. Interest on these set-asides does not accrue until the money is spent, but the set-asides prevent borrowers from taking too much from the line of credit and becoming unable to meet the terms required to stay in the home. These new set-asides grow at the effective rate, not the expected rate used for earlier set-asides, a point whose meaning will become clearer after I explain how reverse mortgages work in the next chapter. This was done to clarify earlier confusion created when set-asides grew at a different rate than everything else.

Concerns should be raised about the viability of an overall retirement income plan when it is necessary to create large set-asides within the line of credit in order to make it work. In some cases, a reverse mortgage might simply be a source of liquidity to cover expenses and allow the borrower to stay in the home while using other limited resources to cover retirement living expenses.

Further Reading

US Dept. of Housing and Urban Development. www.hud.gov. Provides details on HECM rules and contact information for housing counselors.

CHAPTER 4: HOW REVERSE MORTGAGES WORK

The next step to understanding how reverse mortgages fit into retirement income planning is to understand how they work.

Eligibility Requirements for a HECM Borrower

The basic requirements to become an eligible HECM borrower are:

- age (at least sixty-two);
- equity in your home (any existing mortgage can be paid off with loan proceeds);
- financial resources to cover tax, insurance, and maintenance expenses;
- no other federal debt;
- competency; and
- receipt of a counseling certificate from an FHA-approved counselor for attending a personal counseling session on home equity options.

HUD provides a list of approved counselors on its website.

For your property to be eligible, it must:

- serve as your primary residence;
- meet FHA property standards and flood requirements;
- pass an FHA appraisal; and
- be maintained to meet FHA health and safety standards.

If your home does not meet all standards, some home improvements may also be required to initiate a reverse mortgage.

The obligations to pay property taxes, homeowner's insurance, and home maintenance should not be viewed as extraordinary as they are required for any type of mortgage, not just reverse. This protects the lender by keeping up the value of the collateral for the loan.

The Initial Principal Limit: Measuring Available Credit

Reverse mortgages use their own jargon, and it is important to understand the meaning of three key terms: (1) Principal Limit Factor (PLF), (2) expected rate, and (3) effective rate. The last two terms sound similar but work in different ways.

The *principal limit* represents the credit capacity available with a HECM reverse mortgage. We need to understand how to calculate the initial principal limit when the reverse mortgage is opened, as well as how the principal limit grows over time. The initial principal limit is calculated with the *expected rate,* while principal limit growth is calculated with the *effective rate.*

PLFs are published by HUD, with the current version coming out in August 2014. Because HECMs are non-recourse loans, the principal limit that can be borrowed must be less than the home's value to reduce the potential of the loan balance outgrowing it. For this reason, factors are updated over time to manage the risk to the insurance fund.

The basic idea behind reverse mortgages is that the value of the home will eventually be used to repay the loan balance. While the loan balance occasionally ends up exceeding the home's value, the program would be unsustainable if this happened frequently. When the loan balance exceeds the home's appraised value, the insurance fund makes up the difference to protect both the borrower and lender (an important reason insurance premiums exist).

The available credit amount is determined primarily by:

- the appraised home value;
- the homeowner's age (or, for couples, the age of the younger spouse, and one spouse must be at least sixty-two);
- a lender's margin; and
- the 10-year LIBOR swap rate.

Together, the lender's margin and the swap rate add up to the "expected rate."

Expected rate = 10-year LIBOR Swap Rate + Lender's Margin

The PLF determines the borrowing amount as a percentage of the appraised home value, up to the FHA mortgage limit of $625,500. The expected rate is meant to estimate the compounding series of shorter-term interest rates over the next ten years, which provides an estimate for the future path of effective rates. The expected rate is used with the age of the younger spouse to determine the PLF, or the percentage of the home's appraisal value that may be borrowed. If the home's appraisal value exceeds $625,500, this serves as a maximum to which the PLF is applied.

It is important to note that "age" is a bit more complicated than your literal age, since it is rounded up if your birthday falls within six months of the first day of the month in which the loan is closed. For instance, consider someone who is currently sixty-five years old when they close their loan in the month of April. Six months after April 1 is October 1. If this person will be turning sixty-six by the end of September, their age is counted as sixty-six for the purposes of determining the PLF. But if their next birthday is in October or later, the proper age to use for determining the principal limit is sixty-five.

Exhibit 4.1 provides a visual for how these PLFs vary by age and effective rates. The percentage of home value increases when the age of the youngest borrower or non-borrowing spouse is higher and when the expected rate is lower. The PLF is based on a present value calculation: more can be provided initially when the time horizon is shorter and when the discount rate is less.

Exhibit 4.1 Principal Limit Factors: The Percentage of Home Value Initially Available

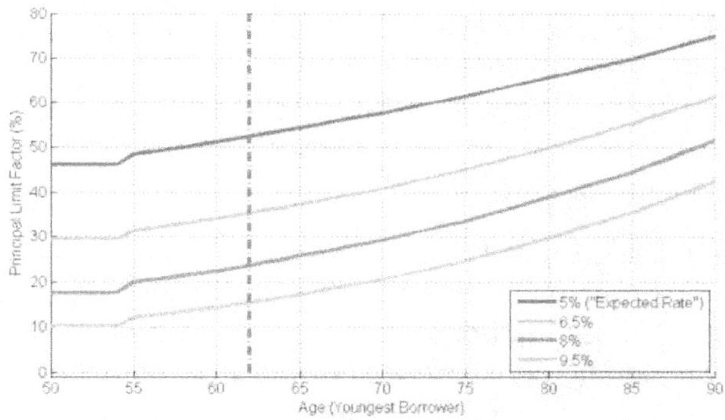

The current low-interest-rate environment provides an advantage when opening a reverse mortgage as the PLF is higher than in the past. Interest rates are much more important than age for determining the PLF. For example, with an expected rate of 5%, the PLF is 50% when the youngest eligible non-borrower is fifty-eight. However, should the rate rise to 6.5%, the youngest borrower would have to be eighty-one before the PLF exceeds 50%. If the expected rate is 6%, the PLF reaches 50% at age seventy-six. In this case, it takes eighteen years for the age impact to offset a 1% rise in interest rates. Because the expected rate is so important, a future increase in interest rates would quickly counteract any benefits from an increasing age in determining the PLF for a new reverse mortgage contract. Exhibit 4.2 provides a similar perspective, but with age and expected rates swapped on the horizontal axis.

Again, we observe lower principal limit factors when expected rates are higher. Increasing ages support higher principal limit factors across the range of expected rates.

Exhibit 4.2 Principal Limit Factors: The Percentage of Home Value Initially Available

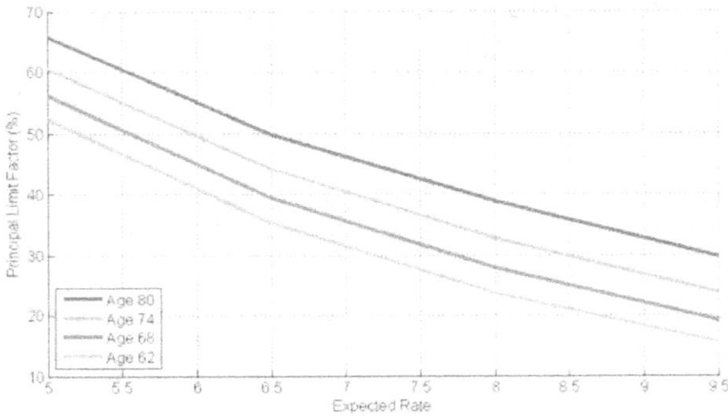

The PLF is the percentage of the home's value initially available. If the principal limit then grows at the "expected rate" thereafter, it is expected to grow to equal the appreciated home value when the loan becomes due (either upon death or leaving the home) using a projected growth rate for home prices similar to the projected overall price inflation rate. This calculation assumes the entire principal limit is borrowed when the loan originates, which is generally no longer possible.

For example, with the current table from August 2014, the PLF is 52.4% when the youngest borrower is sixty-two and the expected rate is 5%. The government's specific assumptions are not provided publicly, but if we assume a 2% growth rate for home appreciation and a remaining life expectancy of 22.3 years, then we can replicate this actual value for the PLF. A home appreciation rate of 2.95% combined with a life expectancy to 100 (thirty-eight years) also makes the calculation work.

The government might use a different combination of values for these two variables, but the below formula shows the basic idea of how the PLF is calculated:

$$PLF = \left(\frac{1 + \text{home value growth rate}}{1 + \text{expected rate}}\right)^{\text{remaining life expectancy}}$$

Upfront Costs for Opening a Reverse Mortgage

Upfront costs for reverse mortgages come in three categories.

1. Origination Fee

First, the mortgage lender can charge an origination fee. Under the HECM program, these fees are currently permitted to be up to 2% of the value for homes worth $200,000 or less. The lender may charge up to $2,500 if this calculation leads to a fee lower than that. For homes worth between $200,000 and $400,000, the maximum allowed origination fee is $4,000 plus 1% of the home's value above $200,000. For homes worth more than $400,000, the maximum origination fee is $6,000.

These fees are the maximum allowed by the government. Lenders with national advertising campaigns may charge the full allowed amounts, as their customers are less likely to engage in comparison shopping and may not recognize these fees as negotiable. Origination charges for smaller lenders may be much less, and some might even provide credits rather than charges for the origination fee as they earn revenue primarily by originating loans to sell on the secondary market rather than through charging origination fees.

I have seen cases in which companies offer total upfront costs of $125 for the required counseling session with a $0 origination fee, along with credits to cover the mortgage insurance and other closing costs described in the following paragraphs. Clearly, shopping around is important. Some lenders also offer lower origination fees for borrowers willing to accept a higher lender's margin.

2. Initial Mortgage Insurance Premium

A second source of upfront costs is the initial mortgage insurance premium paid to the government, which is based on the value of the home. This fee has changed over time. Since October 2013, it has been sitting at 0.5% of the home value (up to $625,500) if the borrower takes out less than 60% of the PLF in the first year, and 2.5% if taking out more than 60% of the PLF in the first year. For those staying under the 60% threshold, the initial mortgage insurance premium is $500 per $100,000 of home value, up to $3,128 for the $625,500 limit.

The purpose of the mortgage insurance premium is to cover the guarantees provided by the FHA to the lender and consumer. This protection ensures the consumer will have access to their full principal limit even if the lender goes out of business, and the lender is protected for the non-recourse aspect of the loan. If the home value cannot cover the loan balance, the government will make up the difference for the lender.

3. Closing Costs

Finally, you have closing costs. These will be similar to closing costs experienced with any type of mortgage. These costs include the FHA-mandated counseling session, home appraisal costs, credit checks, and any costs related to titling. If the appraisal shows shortcomings for the home that could impact health or safety, then additional home repairs may be required as part of setting up the reverse mortgage. A 2011 AARP report estimated that typical closing costs fall into a range of $2,000 to $3,000. This range is also consistent with the numbers found on the calculator created by the National Reverse Mortgage Lenders Association.

The upfront costs could be paid from other resources or financed from the proceeds of the reverse mortgage loan and repaid later with interest. If upfront costs are financed, the remaining net PLF available through the reverse mortgage would be the amount left after subtracting these costs. You should plan to remain in your home for a sufficiently long period to justify payment of any upfront costs.

Securitizing Loans

Readers may wonder how reverse mortgage lenders make money, especially in cases where they credit many of the upfront costs for initiating a mortgage. The answer involves lenders selling the loans to Ginnie Mae for more than the value of the money lent. Ginnie Mae securitizes these loans and sells them to investors, who value these securities for providing government-insured, risk-free returns that, unlike traditional forward mortgages, tend not to be repaid early when interest rates decline.

Ongoing Credit and Costs

The ongoing costs for a reverse mortgage relate to the interest accruing on any outstanding loan balance, as well as any servicing fees. Servicing fees can be up to $35 per month, though they are generally now incorporated into a higher margin rate rather than charged directly to the borrower. Interest on the loan balance grows at the effective rate:

Effective Rate = One-month LIBOR Rate + Lender's Margin + Annual Mortgage Insurance Premium (1.25%)

In January 2016, the one-month LIBOR rate was about 0.4% and the 10-year LIBOR swap rate was about 2.125%. If we assume a 3% lender's margin, that gives us an expected rate of 5.125% and an effective rate of 4.65%:

Expected Rate = 2.125% + 3% = 5.125% (for initial principal limit)

Effective Rate: = 0.4% + 3% + 1.25% = 4.65% (for principal limit growth)

Once determined through the PLF, the initial line of credit grows automatically at a variable rate equal to the lender's margin, a 1.25% mortgage insurance premium (MIP), and subsequent values of one-month or one-year LIBOR rates. These LIBOR rates are the only variable part for future growth, as the lender's margin and MIP are fixed at the beginning. Though the variable rate can be the one-month or one-year LIBOR, in subsequent descriptions I will refer to the one-month LIBOR case. The effective rate is adjusted monthly to reflect updated LIBOR rates. It is capped at ten percentage points above its initial rate. Exhibit 4.3 summarizes how the expected rates and effective rates are calculated and when these rates apply.

Exhibit 4.3 Reverse Mortgage Interest Rates

Type	Components	Applies to:
Expected Rate	10-year LIBOR Swap Rate + Lender's Margin	Initial Principal Limit Factor Set-Asides for Servicing Costs in Old Mortgages
Effective Rate	One-month LIBOR Rate + Lender's Margin + Mortgage Insurance Premium (1.25%)	Ongoing Principal Limit Growth Rate Loan Balance Growth Rate Line of Credit Growth Rate Post-2014 Set-Asides for Financially Strained

The lender's margin rate and ongoing mortgage insurance premium are set contractually at the onset of the loan and cannot change. The margin rate charged on the loan balance is the primary way the lender—or any buyer on the secondary market—earns revenue, especially lenders who have forgone the origination and servicing fees. Estimates for reasonable margin rates are generally between 2.25% and 4%, with higher numbers typically being associated with lower origination and/or servicing costs. Meanwhile, the ongoing mortgage insurance premium helps ensure the government can meet the obligations for the guarantees it supports through the HECM program to both the lenders and borrowers. The government guarantees two things: that the borrower will be able to access their fully entitled line of credit regardless of any financial difficulties on the part of the lender, and that the insurance fund will make the lender whole whenever payment is due and the loan balance exceeds 95% of the appraised value of the home. The government fund also bears the risk with the tenure and term payment options as distributions are guaranteed to continue when the borrower remains in the home, even if the principal limit has been fully tapped.

The insurance premiums protect homeowners from not having to pay back more than the value of the home in cases where the home balance exceeds this value. The lender is protected as well, as the FHA pays the difference in such cases. While this could potentially leave taxpayers on the hook if the mortgage insurance premiums are not sufficient to cover these cases, the government attempts to stay on top of this matter. Mortgage insurance premiums and principal limit factors have been adjusted over time to help keep the system in balance. However, if the option to open a line of credit and leave it unused for many years will grow in popularity, further changes may be needed to keep the mortgage insurance fund sustainable.

Understanding Why and How the HECM Line of Credit Grows

A mortgage's effective rate is applied not just to the loan balance, but also to the overall principal limit, which grows throughout the duration of the loan. How the effective rate is applied may sound technical, but it is an overwhelmingly important point to understand in order to grasp the value of opening a line of credit earlier rather than later.

Typically speaking, the principal limit, loan balance, and remaining line of credit all grow at the same rate. In rare cases in the past, a reverse mortgage included a servicing set-aside that grew at a high enough expected rate that the set-aside balance grew even as expenses were paid, but that is uncommon. As such, a consistent growth rate will be true for all new loans today, since any new set-asides will also grow at the same effective rate.

The sum of the loan balance, line of credit, and any set-aside is the principal limit. Interest and insurance premiums are charged on the loan balance, not on set-asides or the line of credit. Set-asides are not part of the loan balance until they are actually used, but they limit access to the line of credit. Though interest and insurance premiums are not levied on set-asides or the line of credit, both components grow as if interest and premiums were charged.

When funds are borrowed, the line of credit decreases and the loan balance increases. Conversely, voluntary repayments increase the amount of the line of credit, which will then continue to grow at the effective rate, allowing for access to more credit later.

The following equation shows this relationship, which always holds for recent reverse mortgages because all variables in the equation grow at the same effective rate:

Principal Limit = Loan Balance + Available Line of Credit + Set-Asides

Exhibit 4.4 expresses the same concept. The overall principal limit consists of the loan balance, remaining line of credit, and any set-asides. Again, all these factors grow at the same effective rate, which will increase the size of the overall pie over time. If no further spending or repayment happens over time, the proportions of each of these components of the principal limit will remain the same since they all grow at the same rate.

Exhibit 4.4 Components of the Principal Limits

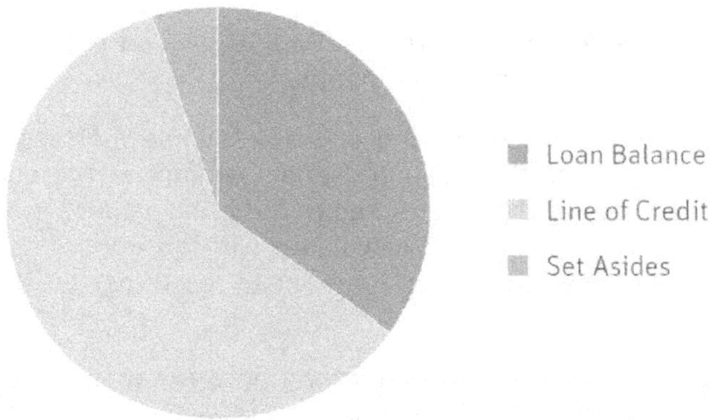

The ability to have an unused line of credit grow is a valuable consideration for opening a reverse mortgage sooner rather than later. It is also a detail that creates a great deal of confusion for those first learning about reverse mortgages, perhaps because it seems this feature is almost too good to be true.

I believe the motivation for the government's design of the HECM reverse mortgage program is based on an underlying assumption that borrowers would spend from their line of credit sooner rather than later, although that is mere speculation. Implicitly, the growth in the principal limit would then reflect growth of the loan balance, more so than the growth of the line of credit. In other words, designers assumed the loan balance would be a large percentage of the principal limit.

The line of credit happens to grow at the same rate as the loan balance, and, if left unused, the line of credit could grow to be quite large. There was probably not much expectation that individuals would open lines of credit and then leave them alone for long periods of time. However, as will be discussed, the bulk of the research on this matter since 2012 suggests this sort of delayed gradual use of the line of credit can be extremely helpful in prolonging the longevity of an investment portfolio.

A simple example may help illuminate the concept further. Consider two individuals. Each opens a reverse mortgage with a principal limit of $100,000. For simplicity's sake, we'll assume that ten years later, the principal limit for both borrowers has grown to $200,000.

Person A takes out the entire $100,000 initially from the reverse mortgage (100% of the principal limit is the loan balance). For Person A, the $200,000 principal limit after ten years reflects a $200,000 loan balance (the loan balance is still 100% of the principal limit), which consists of the initial $100,000 they received plus another $100,000 divided between accumulated interest payments and insurance premiums.

Person B takes a different route and opens a reverse mortgage but does not use any of the credit, so the $200,000 principal limit at the end of ten years fully reflects the value of the line of credit. The principal limit was still 100% in the line of credit. This value was calculated with an implicit assumption that interest and insurance payments have been accruing, even though they haven't.

Person B can then take out the full $200,000 after ten years and have the same loan balance as Person A, but Person B has received $200,000 rather than $100,000. At this point, Person B has bypassed the accumulation of interest and insurance, to the detriment of the lender and the mortgage insurance fund.

Another question that will arise: Would the line of credit ultimately be larger if opened early on rather than waiting until later to open it? We can further explore this question with a more realistic type of example. Exhibit 4.5 below provides an illustration of the impact of opening the reverse mortgage at different points in time using a few basic assumptions.

Exhibit 4.5 Comparing Principal Limits Based on When the Reverse Mortgage Opens

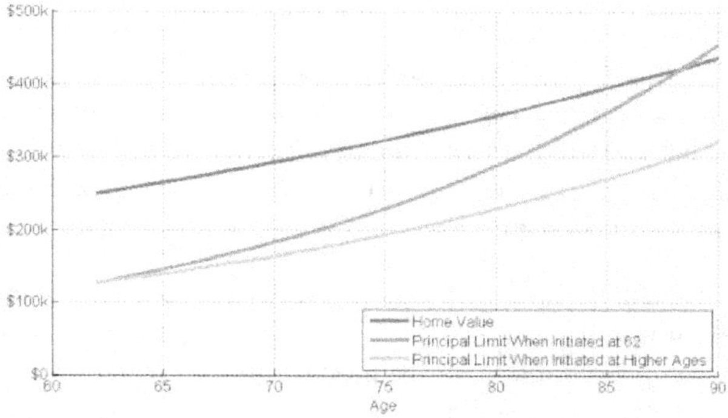

Still keeping matters relatively simple, I assume the one-month LIBOR rate stays permanently at 0.4% and the 10-year LIBOR swap rate remains permanently at 2.125%. The lender's margin is assumed to be 3%, and home inflation is 2%.

For a sixty-two-year-old with a home worth $250,000 today, the exhibit charts three values over time until the individual is ninety. The home value grows by 2% annually, and it is worth $435,256 by age ninety. The principal limit for a reverse mortgage opened at sixty-two is $127,000 (based on a principal limit factor of 50.8% for the 5.125% expected rate. The principal limit grows at an effective rate of 4.65%, and the principal limit is worth $453,421 by age ninety.

At ninety, the principal limit has actually exceeded the value of the home. As a side note, if this principal limit was reflected as a loan balance instead of a line of credit, the loan is non-recourse and the amount due by the borrower cannot exceed the home's value—this is a guarantee supported by insurance premiums.

Finally, Exhibit 4.5 also shows the available principal limit if the reverse mortgage is not opened until each subsequent age, rather than at age sixty-two. By delaying the start of the reverse mortgage and assuming the expected rate of 5.125% remains, the principal limit grows because the principal limit factor is higher at advanced ages, and because this factor is applied to a higher home value.

Nonetheless, even at age ninety, the available principal limit for a new reverse mortgage is only $320,784, which is based on a PLF of 73.7% applied to a higher home value. The overwhelming message from this example is that opening the line of credit early allows for a much greater availability of future credit relative than waiting to open the reverse mortgage later in retirement.

This example assumes that interest rates remain low, but if interest rates were to increase in the future, the value of opening the line of credit today would be even greater. With lower rates today, the available PLF is currently higher. Then, higher future interest rates would cause the effective rate to be higher, so the principal limit grows more quickly. Rising rates would also increase to the expected rate used to calculate principal limits on new reverse mortgages in the future. This would reduce the principal limit on newly issued future loans.

Only extreme growth in home prices could possibly allow more credit to be obtained by delaying the start of a reverse mortgage, but higher home price growth would surely be caused by higher inflation, which would also increase interest rates and reduce the future PLF. It seems to be a relative certainty that more credit will be available in the future by starting the reverse mortgage as soon as possible rather than waiting to open it later.

All of this may sound too good to be true, and it probably is to some extent. Perhaps this is why it is difficult to grasp the concept of line of credit growth throughout retirement. I've already noted that unused lines of credit work for borrowers to the detriment of lenders and the government insurance fund. Such use of a reverse mortgage still exists today and would be contractually protected for those who initiate reverse mortgages under the current rules. At some point in the future, I expect to see new limitations about line of credit growth, especially as more people start to follow the findings of recent research on this matter.

Line of credit growth may be viewed a bit like an unintended loophole that is strengthened by our low interest rate environment. The rules will probably be changed someday for newly issued loans. Until then, research points to this growth as a valuable way reverse mortgages can contribute to a retirement income plan.

Reverse Mortgage Calculator

At https://www.retirementresearcher.com/reverse-mortgage-calculator, I have created a calculator that allows users to get a sense of the principal limit available with a HECM reverse mortgage on their home using the most popular one-month variable rate option. A preview of the calculator is shown in Exhibit 4.6. The calculator asks for eight boxed inputs and uses these inputs to calculate the net principal limit. The calculator also provides the amount of cash flow that could be received as a tenure payment for those seeking this option. An optional ninth input also allows a term payment amount to be calculated. I will describe tenure and term payments in detail later, but the calculator provides sufficient definitions for now.

The first input is the *Home's Appraised Value.* This value is then compared with the $625,500 FHA lending limit to determine the *HECM eligible amount* (the eligible amount is the lesser of the two). The next two inputs are the current *10-year LIBOR Swap Rate* and the *Lender's Margin,* which together comprise the expected rate. The next input is the *Age of Youngest Eligible (Borrower or Non-Borrower) Spouse.* The four inputs thus far are used to calculate the *Principal Limit Factor.* Next, inputs for Loan *Origination Fee* and *Other Closing Costs* are combined with the predetermined cost for the *Initial Mortgage Insurance* premium to determine the total upfront loan cost.

The seventh input asks for the *Percentage of Upfront Costs* to be Financed by the loan. This would be 0% if costs are financed from other resources, 100% if fully financed by the loan, or any number in between. The final input is the amount of *Debt Repayment, Repairs, or Other Life-Expectancy Set-Aside Requirements (LESA)* that have been determined as part of the new financial assessments for borrowers. This information about costs and set-asides is then applied to the eligible home value and the PLF to calculate the net available HECM credit with the loan.

Finally, the calculator provides the net amounts available as either tenure or term payments. The tenure payment is calculated assuming a planning horizon of age 100 and the expected rate plus the ongoing mortgage insurance premium. The term payment is calculated for a fixed term, though if the desired number of years for the term payment should extend beyond age 100, the term payment is automatically adjusted to be the higher value of the tenure payment. Tenure and term payments are both provided as monthly and annual values, and the tenure payment is also represented as a payout rate based on a percentage of the net principal limit plus the financed upfront costs.

Exhibit 4.6 HECM Calculator: Net Available Line of Credit or Tenure Payment for a Variable Rate Loan

HECM 4 Nevers

In her book What's the Deal with Reverse Mortgages?, Shelley Giordano describes what she calls the "HECM 4 Nevers" to help alleviate common misconceptions of the program. She clarifies that homeowners never give up the title to their home; never owe more than the home's value upon leaving the home; never have to leave the home due to spending down their line of credit as long as taxes, insurance, and home maintenance continue; and never have to make loan repayments in advance of leaving the home unless you choose to do so.

Deciding on a Package of Costs for a HECM Reverse Mortgage

The discussion of reverse mortgage costs has several moving parts. Which type of cost combination to choose depends on how you plan to use the line of credit during retirement. Let me reveal the punchline for the following discussion: Those seeking to spend the credit quickly will benefit more from a cost package with higher upfront costs and a lower lender's margin rate. Meanwhile, those seeking to open a line of credit that may go unused for many years could find better opportunities with a package of costs that trades lower upfront costs for a slightly higher lender's margin rate. However, the reduction in the initial PLF caused by a higher lender's margin generally means a lower lender's margin is potentially worth paying for, if necessary, in terms of a higher upfront cost. These cases must be considered carefully.

To summarize the cost discussion, costs determined by the lender include:

- Origination fees
- Other closing costs
- Servicing Fees
- Margin Rate

Along with the upfront mortgage insurance premium, which the lender does not control (though some lenders may provide a credit to cover it), the upfront costs include the origination fees and other typical closing costs. The maximum that can be charged for origination fees is set by the government and relates to the home's value, as described before. Lenders have discretion to charge less than this amount. Smaller lenders with smaller marketing budgets may compete more on price, which can include a lower origination fee, or even credits to offset other fees.

For other closing costs, these fees vary and relate to the typical costs for opening a mortgage (e.g., titling and appraisal charges) as well as payment for the mandatory counseling session. Some lenders may also provide credits to cover these costs as well. As for servicing fees, lenders are allowed to charge up to $35 per month, but recently it is common not to charge an explicit servicing fee, and instead include the servicing fees as part of the lender's margin rate.

The final cost to consider is the lender's margin rate. This is not an upfront cost but an ongoing cost charged to the outstanding loan balance. The choice of lender's margin is important because it affects both the initial PLF and the subsequent growth rate of the principal limit. A higher lender's margin reduces the initial principal limit as part of the expected rate, but this principal limit subsequently grows faster as the margin is also part of the effective rate that determines principal limit growth.

The lender's margin is part of the expected rate, and a higher lender's margin implies a higher expected rate, which in turn implies a lower principal limit factor. For example, if the 10-year LIBOR swap rate is 2.125%, a sixty-two-year-old with a $400,000 home could see his initial principal limit fall from $203,200 to $153,600 by choosing a 4% lender's margin instead of a 3% lender's margin. This represents a reduction in the principal limit factor from 50.8% to 38.4%.

The lender's margin is also included as a variable to determine the effective rate—the rate at which the principal limit grows. Remember that the effective rate also defines the rate of growth for both the outstanding loan balance and the remaining line of credit. Those with a small loan balance would like a high lender's margin because it will allow their line of credit to grow more quickly, while those with a large loan balance— everything else being the same—would prefer a lower lender's margin so the loan balance does not grow as quickly.

These four ingredients can be combined into different packages by the lender. The best choice depends on how the reverse mortgage is used. When funds will be extracted earlier, it may be worthwhile to pay higher upfront fees coupled with a lower margin rate. However, for the standby line of credit, which may go untapped, it could be beneficial to lean toward a higher margin rate combined with a package for reduced origination and servicing fees. Some lenders may even offer credits to cover most of the upfront fees.

Keep in mind, though, that while a higher lender's margin will allow the line of credit to grow more quickly, the initial line of credit value will be smaller because the PLF will be smaller. If the choice for a higher lender's margin is not compensated by sufficiently lower upfront fees, then the number of years required for the line of credit to grow to offset the initial deficiency may be too great. This is illustrated in Exhibit 4.7, for a case of a sixty-two-year-old borrower with a 10-year LIBOR swap rate of 2.125% and a one-month LIBOR rate that stays at 0.4%. Though the line of credit grows faster with the 4% margin, it has still not caught up to the value of the line of credit with a 3% margin by age ninety.

Exhibit 4.7 Comparing Line of Credit Growth with Different Lender's Margins

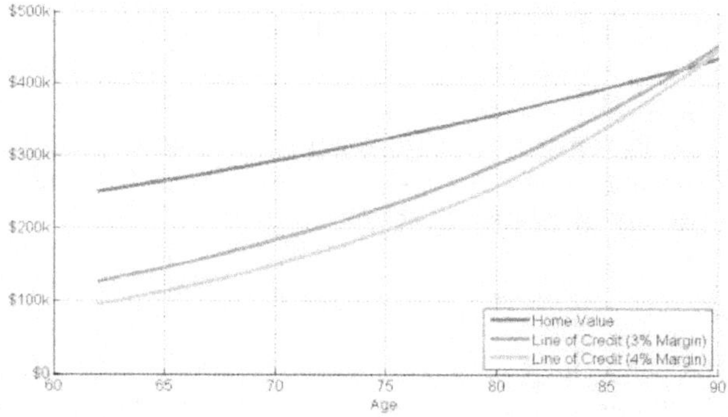

Repayment of the HECM Loan Balance

Repayment of a HECM loan balance may be deferred until the last borrower or non-borrowing spouse has died, moved, or sold the home. Prior to that time, repayments can be made voluntarily at any point with no penalty for early repayment to help reduce future interest due and allow for a larger line of credit to grow for subsequent use.

When the final repayment is due, the title for the home remains with the borrower or estate. Should beneficiaries wish to keep the home, the loan balance can be repaid with other funds. Heirs could also refinance the home with a traditional mortgage should they wish to keep it. If they decide to sell the home, they keep anything beyond the outstanding loan balance. Should the loan balance exceed what the home can reasonably be sold for, heirs can simply give the home to the lender through a deed in lieu of foreclosure without worrying about selling it themselves. However, they may be sacrificing a large interest deduction on their taxes if they do this.

A deed in lieu of foreclosure is sufficient to extinguish the debt on the reverse mortgage—mortgage insurance from the government will compensate the lender for the difference. Generally, the borrower or heirs have up to 360 days to sell the home or refinance when the loan comes due, but this requires a few extensions from the lender. If you intend to use the full 360 days, it is essential that you maintain regular contact and provide updates to the lender during that time.

Tax Issues

Distributions from reverse mortgages are treated as loan advances and do not reflect taxable income. They are not included in adjusted gross income and do not impact Medicare premiums or the taxation of Social Security benefits. In this regard, proceeds from a reverse mortgage behave the same way as Roth IRA distributions. They can provide a way to increase spending power without pushing you into a higher tax bracket.

A more complex area relates to eligible deductions for reverse mortgages. These taxation issues for reverse mortgages can be complex and are still relatively untested and not fully addressed in the tax code. Researchers Barry Sacks and Tom Davison have recently been exploring deeper into the tax code to better understand these aspects (see further reading). Individual cases vary, so a tax professional with reverse mortgage experience should always be consulted.

Interest charges, mortgage insurance premiums, and possibly real estate taxes may be accumulated as part of the loan balance and may not be repaid until many years later. These are all potentially deductible at different points in time, either as they are incurred or when repaid.

Davison has spent a good deal of time exploring IRS publications about these issues, which he has written up at his *Tools for Retirement Planning* blog. He notes that interest can generally not be deducted on taxes until it is actually repaid. Interest payments include interest charged on the borrowed amount and interest compounded on past interest charged. These two aspects of interest may be treated differently for taxes, as interest on interest is not addressed in tax rules.

Repayments on the loan balance are first applied to mortgage insurance premiums, then servicing fees, interest, and then principal amounts borrowed. So repayment cannot lead to interest deductions until the MIP and servicing fee components have been fully repaid. Interest due on the loan balance can potentially be large, so this is an important aspect of tax planning to make sure the repayment timing allows for the best use of this deduction.

Mortgage insurance premiums can be tax deductible if the borrowing reflects acquisition debt. This is a reverse mortgage use for buying, building, or substantially improving a home. The HECM for Purchase program, as well as major home improvement projects, should qualify under this criterion. Mortgage insurance premiums are deductible when they are paid by the borrower. There are also income limits for the deduction, as the AGI for a couple filing jointly must be less than $100,000 for a full deduction and

$109,000 for a partial deduction. Also, the ability to deduct these insurance premiums is not a permanent part of the tax code, and it needs to be extended each year to remain. The deductible still exists as of 2016. Finally, in cases when real estate taxes are paid from the line of credit, perhaps with a life-expectancy set aside requirement, the deduction for these taxes should happen as they are incurred rather than repaid.

HELOC vs. HECM

Both a traditional home equity line of credit (HELOC – pronounced as "he-lock") and a HECM can serve as a source for contingency funds in retirement, but they cannot be combined on a given home. Important differences must be considered between the two options. People often think they should just use a HELOC and not bother with a HECM. The differences between the two should be considered before taking either one.

With a HELOC, repayments are required sooner. Users of a HECM can voluntarily repay sooner but are under no obligation to make any repayment before leaving the home.

In addition, retirees may not qualify for a HELOC if they do not have regular income. Though HECMs added new safeguards in 2015 to make sure they are not solely used as a last resort by those who have otherwise depleted their resources, the qualification requirements are less stringent than with a HELOC. A HECM may still be available with set-asides included to cover tax, insurance, and maintenance obligations. In addition, initial start-up costs may differ for the two options.

A HECM also differs from a HELOC in that its line of credit cannot be cancelled, frozen, or reduced. This was such a large problem with HELOCs during the 2008 financial crisis. With a HECM, borrowers are protected from lenders modifying their obligations to lend remaining funds in the line of credit. No such protections are available with HELOCs. The principal limit for a HECM will also grow throughout retirement, unlike the fixed amount available with a HELOC.

In contrast to a HELOC, the HECM is non-cancellable, the borrower controls if and when it is used, it has flexible payback control, and the line of credit grows over time independent of home value. If your goal is to set up a liquid contingency fund, a number of important differences must be examined between HECMs and HELOCs.

Further Reading

Davison, Tom, and Keith Turner. 2015. "The Reverse Mortgage: A Strategic Lifetime Planning Resource." *Journal of Retirement* 3, 2 (Fall): 61-79.

Davison, Tom. 2016. "Tax Deductions and Reverse Mortgages." *Tools for Retirement Planning* blog. [Link]

Giordano, Shelley. 2015. *What's the Deal With Reverse Mortgages?* Pennington, NJ: People Tested Media. [Link]

Sacks, Barry H., Nicholas Miningas, Stephen R. Sacks, and Francis Vitagliano.2016. "Recovering a Lost Deduction." *Journal of Taxation* 124, 4 (April): 157-169.

CHAPTER 5: POTENTIAL USES FOR A REVERSE MORTGAGE

A reverse mortgage can fit into a retirement income plan in several ways, but it is important to first understand your options for taking them out. Most current HECM reverse mortgages use an adjustable interest rate, which allows the proceeds from the reverse mortgage to be taken out in any of four ways.

The spending options for a variable-rate HECM reverse mortgage include:

1. Lump-Sum Payment: Take out a large amount initially, though not necessarily the full amount available. As I've mentioned before, the government discourages taking out more than 60% of the available credit within the first year by charging a higher mortgage insurance premium on the eligible home value (2.5% instead of 0.5%) when this is done. Taking out more than 60% of available credit is only allowed in a few specific circumstances, such as paying down an existing mortgage or using the HECM for Purchase.

2. Tenure Payment: Works similarly to an income annuity with a fixed monthly payment guaranteed to be received as long as the borrower remains in the home (which, to be clear, is not the same as dying, as the borrower may leave the home while still alive). Tenure payments allow for additional spending from the reverse mortgage even when the line of credit has been fully used. The mortgage insurance fund bears the risk that payouts and loan growth from the tenure payment option exceed the subsequent value of the home when the loan becomes due.

The available monthly tenure payment can be calculated using the PMT formula in Excel:

=PMT(rate, nper, pv, 0, 1)

• In which *rate* is the expected rate plus the 1.25% mortgage insurance premium, all divided by twelve to convert into a monthly amount. This gives us the rate the loan balance is expected to grow. For example, a 5% expected rate makes this number 6.25%/12 = 0.521%.

• *nper* is the number of months between the age of the youngest borrower (or eligible non-borrowing spouse) and age 100. For example, a new sixty-two-year-old has 456 months (thirty-eight years) until he or she turns 100.

• And *pv* is the net principal limit from the reverse mortgage. It is found by multiplying the principal limit factor by the appraised value of the home (up to $625,500) less any upfront costs financed with the loan or any set-asides. For instance, a sixty-two-year-old with a $500,000 home and a 52.4% principal limit who pays upfront costs from other resources will have a $262,000 net principal limit.

And so, PMT (6.25%/12, 456, 262000, 0, 1) = $1,498 for a monthly tenure payment. Annually, this adds up to $17,972 from the reverse mortgage.

My reverse mortgage calculator at www.retirementresearcher.com/reverse-mortgage-calculator also provides these calculations for tenure payments.

3. Term Payment: A fixed monthly payment is received for a fixed amount of time. Calculating a term payment is similar to calculating a tenure payment. The only difference is that *nper* will be smaller, as it is the desired number of months the term payment should last. If the number of months pushed the term past age 100, a tenure payment would be used instead. As with a tenure payment, the full amount of term payments will be paid even if rising rates cause the loan balance plus new payments to exceed the principal limit.

As an example, consider an eight-year term payment, which could

be used as part of a strategy to delay Social Security. The monthly term payment would be PMT (6.25%/12, 8*12, 262000, 0, 1) = $3,457, or $41,484 annually.

4. Line of Credit: Home equity does not need to be spent initially, or ever. A number of strategies involve opening a line of credit and then leaving it to grow at a variable interest rate as an available asset to cover a variety of contingencies later in retirement. Distributions can be taken from the remaining line of credit whenever desired until the line of credit has been used in its entirety.

Some of these spending options can be combined.

Using a portion of the line of credit to create tenure or term payments and leaving the remainder to grow is called "modified tenure" and "modified term." You can also change spending options over time, in which case updated term or tenure payments would be based on the available line of credit. Should tenure or term payments begin at a later date, the expected rate used to calculate the initial principal limit would remain the same throughout the term of the loan.

Potential Uses for a HECM Reverse Mortgage

Now that we understand how reverse mortgages work, we can go into greater depth on the potential ways a HECM reverse mortgage can be used within a retirement income plan. For instance, it could be used:

- as a backup source for liquidity and spending,
- as an annuity alternative, or
- as a hedge to protect the value of one's home.

The following table provides an organizational framework for thinking about potential uses. They are ordered from uses that spend available credit more quickly to those that may never tap the line of credit.

Exhibit 5.1 groups the uses into four general categories of how reverse mortgages are often utilized:

- debt coordination for housing;
- portfolio coordination for retirement spending;
- a resource to fund retirement income strategy enhancements;
- as insurance for various retirement contingencies.

Later chapters will provide more details on many of these topics, but I will not cover some extensively—mostly in the retirement efficiency improvements category, which in practice can be difficult to distinguish from portfolio coordination for retirement spending.

A HECM reverse mortgage could be used as a potential additional funding source to opportunities that may enhance an overall retirement plan without placing undue additional pressures on the investment portfolio.

Exhibit 5.1 The Spectrum of Reverse Mortgage Uses

Categories	Examples
Portfolio/Debt Coordination for Housing	Pay off an Existing Mortgage
	Transition from Traditional Mortgage to Reverse Mortgage
	Fund Home Renovations to Allow for Aging in Place
	HECM for Purchase for New Home
Portfolio Coordination for Retirement Spending	Spend Home Equity First to Leverage Portfolio Upside Potential
	Coordinate HECM Spending to Mitigate Sequence Risk
	Use Tenure Payments to Reduce Portfolio Withdrawals
Funding Source for Retirement Efficiency Improvements	Tenure Payments as Annuity Alternative
	Social Security Delay Bridge
	Tax Bracket Management or Pay Taxes for Roth Conversions
	Pay Premiums for Existing Long Term Care Insurance Policy
Preserve Credit as Insurance Policy	Support Retirement Spending After Portfolio Depletion
	Protective Hedge for Home Value
	Provides Contingency Fund for Spending Shocks (In home care, health expenses, divorce settlement)

Though it may not always be possible to fully differentiate these uses from coordinated spending with the portfolio, the idea of creating this separate category is to illustrate possibilities beyond portfolio spending that can allow for greater retirement efficiency.

A reverse mortgage may be a helpful resource to engage in certain long-term strategies that might otherwise be less obtainable, such as:

• to create a Social Security Delay Bridge,

• to pay for the taxes to enable Roth conversions in the years prior to required minimum distributions,

• to otherwise help manage falling into a higher than necessary tax bracket, or

• to maintain a long-term care insurance policy by paying insurance

premiums from the line of credit or by treating tenure payments as an alternative to using an income annuity.

For those with sufficient assets who could afford to fund these retirement efficiencies with their investment portfolios, the matter becomes determining the direction that can provide the most attractive distribution of overall outcomes for the retirement plan. Applying these sorts of strategies would become a subset of general uses for a HECM to support retirement spending.

These strategies may have the biggest impact for typical Americans approaching age sixty-two with few financial assets and most of their net worth tied up in their home. For example, those with a small enough investment portfolio and who cannot work past sixty-two may not otherwise be able to afford to delay Social Security. Home equity could provide a way to build that bridge to Social Security delay. For some individuals, though, the available principal limit from the reverse mortgage may be insufficient to support eight years of age seventy benefits, or even age sixty-two benefits. There would be also be an important tradeoff to consider, as the housing asset on the balance sheet would be diminished to fund Social Security delay, which leaves fewer contingency assets available to the household. The guaranteed lifetime income stream supported through Social Security would be dramatically enhanced though. It would be important to explore these possibilities and tradeoffs on a case-by-case basis to determine the best course of action.

CHAPTER 6: PORTFOLIO COORDINATION FOR RETIREMENT SPENDING

Maintaining higher fixed costs in retirement increases exposure to sequence risk by requiring a higher withdrawal rate from remaining assets. Drawing from a reverse mortgage has the potential to mitigate this aspect of sequence risk by reducing the need for portfolio withdrawals either generally, or just at inopportune times.

A HECM line of credit provides a tool that can be used to mitigate the impacts of sequence of returns risk. Since 2012, a series of research articles has highlighted how the strategic use of a reverse mortgage can either preserve greater overall legacy wealth for a given spending goal, or otherwise sustain a higher spending amount for longer in retirement (see "Further Reading" at the end of this chapter).

The conventional wisdom on how to treat housing wealth in retirement was to preserve it as a last resort option. If it did not need to be used, the home may be left as part of the legacy for the next generation.

However, starting in 2012, a series of articles published in the *Journal of Financial Planning* investigated how obtaining a HECM reverse mortgage early in retirement and then strategically spending from the available credit can help improve the sustainability of retirement income strategies.

We can think of legacy wealth at death as the combined value of any remaining financial assets plus the remaining home equity once the reverse mortgage loan balance has been repaid:

Legacy Wealth = Remaining Financial Assets + [Home Equity – minimum(Loan Balance, 95% of Appraised Home Value)]

If we do not worry about the percentage breakdown between these two categories, research reveals the possibility of sustaining a spending goal while also leaving a larger legacy at death. Strategically using home equity can lead to a more efficient strategy than the less flexible option of viewing the home as the legacy asset that must not be touched until everything else is gone. This analysis provides a way to test whether the costs of the reverse mortgage—in terms of the upfront costs and compounding growth of the loan balance—are outweighed by the benefits of mitigating sequence risk. Strategic use of a reverse mortgage line of credit is shown to improve retirement sustainability, despite the costs, without adversely impacting legacy wealth.

Based on his personal research going as far back as 2004, Barry Sacks got the ball rolling and received widespread recognition for ideas presented in a research article he published with his brother Stephen in the February 2012 issue of the *Journal of Financial Planning.* Barry Sacks is to supplementing retirement spending with a reverse mortgage line of credit as William Bengen is to the 4% rule. He was thinking over a decade ago about how people could use housing wealth as a type of volatility buffer to help mitigate sequence of returns risk.

The aptly named article these brothers wrote—"Reversing the Conventional Wisdom: Using Home Equity to Supplement Retirement Income"—set out to present the reverse mortgage option as something more than a last resort.

The title states their objective clearly. They investigated sustainable withdrawal rates from an investment portfolio coupled with home equity to determine whether asset depletion takes place when using three different strategies for incorporating home equity into the retirement income plan:

1. Use a reverse mortgage as a last resort to continue spending only after the investment portfolio is depleted (i.e., the conventional wisdom).

2. Open a reverse mortgage line of credit at the start of retirement and spend it down first, then transition to using portfolio withdrawals for the remainder of retirement.

3. Open a reverse mortgage line of credit at the start of retirement and draw from it during any years that follow a negative return for the investment portfolio. This is their "coordinated strategy."

They reversed the conventional wisdom by using Monte Carlo simulations to quantify how spending strategies (2) and (3) enjoyed a higher probability for success and could be sustained longer than (1).

They also found the remaining net worth of the household (the value of their remaining financial portfolio plus any remaining home equity) after thirty years of retirement is twice as likely to be larger with an alternative strategy than with the conventional wisdom of saving home equity to be used last.

For withdrawal rate goals between 4.5% and 7% of the initial retirement date portfolio balance, the residual net worth after thirty years was 67% to 75% more likely to be higher with a coordinated strategy than with a strategy using the reverse mortgage as a last resort. In other words, spending home equity did not ruin the possibility for leaving an inheritance. Instead, the opposite was true.

How is this the case? Essentially, scenarios (2) and (3) provide a cushion against the dreaded sequence of returns risk that is such a fundamental challenge to building a sustainable retirement plan. When home equity is used last, retirees are spending down their volatile investment portfolio earlier in retirement and are more exposed to locking in portfolio losses, more easily leading them on the path to depletion.

With option (2), if home equity is spent first, the financial portfolio is left alone in the interim, providing a better chance to grow so that by the time home equity is spent, retirees will be able to continue a given spending amount in their retirement using what is likely be a lower withdrawal rate from a now larger portfolio. They quantify that the costs and interest paid on the reverse mortgage, while substantial, are less than the benefits the strategy provides to retirees and their beneficiaries.

And option (3) provides a more sophisticated technique to grapple with sequence of returns risk by only spending from the reverse mortgage line of credit when the retiree is vulnerable to locking in portfolio losses: spend from the line of credit only after years in which the financial portfolio has declined.

Sacks and Sacks make clear that their point is not that all retirees should take a reverse mortgage, but that retirees who wish to remain in their homes for as long as possible should view it as more than a last resort. If a retiree decides to spend at a higher level, which could lead to portfolio depletion and then possibly require them to also generate cash flows from their home equity, there is indeed a better way.

In a sign that the time had finally come for the idea of coordinated spending from a reverse mortgage, Harold Evensky, Shaun Pfeiffer, and John Salter of Texas Tech University followed suit with two articles—beginning with the August 2012 issue of the *Journal of Financial Planning*—investigating the role of a standby line of credit. They developed conclusions quite similar to the Sacks brothers without knowing of their work.

Harold Evensky said the motivation for their research came about when the home equity line of credit (HELOC) he had established as a source of liquidity for his clients kept getting cancelled during the financial crisis in 2008. The reverse mortgage line of credit was guaranteed to be there even in times of market stress. They write, "Although reverse mortgages aren't for everyone, the reluctance to consider use of reverse mortgages in the distribution phase limits the flexibility of distribution strategies."

Their first article in 2012 investigated the use of a HECM Saver line of credit (which, you may recall, had lower costs but was later merged with the HECM Standard in September 2013) as a ready source of cash to be used as a risk management tool for retirement distributions. The purpose of their research was in line with that of Sacks and Sacks: to test portfolio sustainability using Monte Carlo simulations when portfolio distributions are coordinated with a reverse mortgage.

With a similar objective in mind, they developed a coordinated strategy to better approximate using the reverse mortgage when the portfolio was in jeopardy. Rather than drawing from the reverse mortgage standby line of credit after years of market downturns, they instead drew from the line of credit whenever the remaining portfolio balance fell below the value indicated by a separate wealth glide path calculation. They determined the amount of remaining wealth required for each year of retirement to keep the spending plan on a sustainable path through the desired planning horizon. After experimenting with this critical path for remaining wealth, they determined that drawing from the reverse mortgage worked best when remaining wealth fell to less than 80% of the wealth glide path. This helped avoid overuse of the line of credit while still providing a mechanism to avoid selling financial assets at overly depreciated prices, thereby helping mitigate the sequence of returns risk.

Another difference between this research and that of the Sacks brothers is that whenever remaining wealth grew enough to be back above the 80% barrier for their critical path trajectory, Evensky & co. worked to preserve a larger line of credit for future use by paying back any outstanding balance on the line of credit throughout retirement. This contrasted Sacks and Sacks, who made no voluntary repayment during retirement.

Evensky has heralded the value of using cash reserves to mitigate sequence risk since the 1980s. Cash provides a drag on potential portfolio returns, but its presence serves as an alternative choice to finance spending and avoid selling other assets at a loss. He suggested having two years of spending in a separate bucket and investing remaining funds with a total returns investment perspective. He viewed this as a compromise between the offsetting factors of the drag on returns created by holding more cash and not completely protecting the remaining portfolio if market declines lasted longer than two years.

The reverse mortgage research of these two articles follows along the same path with the line of credit used in place of a larger cash reserve. In the 2012 article, they replaced the two-year cash reserve with a six-month cash reserve, and they used the line of credit to refill the reserve when necessary in order to reduce the cash drag and provide a source of funds not impacted by declining market returns, which allows funding to last substantially longer than two years.

Their glide path approach to choosing when to tap the line of credit establishes decision rules that keep better track of cumulative outcomes, so it makes intuitive sense. Their 2012 research uses the line of credit as a source of funds only when the portfolio is below the mark set by the glide path *and* the cash reserve bucket has been depleted.

As with Sacks and Sacks, they found that using the standby line of credit improved portfolio survival without creating an adverse impact on median remaining wealth (including remaining home equity). This provided independent confirmation that the reverse mortgage line of credit can help mitigate sequence of returns risk without impacting legacy goals. They also confirmed that having a larger line of credit (either through a higher PLF with lower interest rates or greater home value) relative to the portfolio size heightens the likelihood of sustaining a positive portfolio balance. As a result, these strategies were shown to be more attractive in low interest rate environments. Evensky & co. conclude that a standby line of credit deserves a role in mainstream retirement income planning for four reasons:

1. it diminishes the need to maintain a larger cash buffer,

2. it provides flexibility to hold onto investments during bear markets,

3. it allows flexibility to use home equity as a source of spending, and

4. it improves portfolio survivorship rates without an adverse impact on remaining legacy wealth.

In December 2013, the same authors returned with a second study on using a standby line of credit for retirement income planning. This time, they shifted the focus to how much the sustainable withdrawal rate could be increased with a line of credit while maintaining a 90% success rate over a thirty-year retirement. They confirm that the standby line of credit helps sustain higher withdrawal rates when retirement starts in a low-interest-rate environment and/or the home is worth more than the investment portfolio.

Consistent with other withdrawal rate research using lower capital

market expectations than the historical average, they calculate that the sustainable spending rate without a reverse mortgage is 3.25%. With a reverse mortgage, the withdrawal rate can reach 6.5%. This highest number happens when the home value matches the portfolio size and interest rates are low at the start of retirement. Since the HECM Saver no longer existed on its own, this article considered the new form, which still exists today.

Otherwise, assumptions are the same as their previous article. They note that these higher withdrawal rates are on par with those obtained through dynamic spending strategies that can involve substantial spending reductions over time, but that the HECM strategy can sustain the higher spending rate without such reductions.

Bringing the Reverse Mortgage Tenure Payment Option to the Forefront

December 2013 was a busy month for research articles on reverse mortgages in the *Journal of Financial Planning.* The other published that month was Gerald Wagner's "The 6.0 Percent Rule." Based on the title alone, it would seem that the article only provides a further confirmation for the previous research that strategic use of a line of credit can enhance sustainability for higher spending rates.

However, this article provides an important further detail to the research to earn its place in the apex of this first generation of research from 2012-2013. Wagner contributes the idea that when there is an upward sloping yield curve for interest rates (interest rates for long-term bonds are higher than for short-term bonds), setting up term or tenure payments with a reverse mortgage is even more effective than drawing down a line of credit in other ways. The tenure and term payments are based on a higher assumed interest rate with the 10-year LIBOR swap rate (plus the same lender's margin and mortgage insurance premium as with line of credit

growth), while the line of credit will grow at a rate based on the lower one-month LIBOR swap rate as the variable component.

If we assume one-month LIBOR rates stay at their current levels, sustainable withdrawals over a fixed term can be calculated in the same way as a term payment. Excel's PMT function uses the same inputs as a term payment calculation except the lower one-month rate instead of the higher 10-year rate. This results in less spending from the line of credit. For spending rates up to 6%, different uses of term or tenure payments support the highest sustainable spending rates over retirement. This result is dependent on an upward sloping yield curve and short-term interest rates remaining sufficiently low. An inverted yield curve or rapidly rising short-term rates could allow for greater sustainable spending from the line of credit.

Term and tenure payments provide a different view of the line of credit. They provide fixed, ongoing payments for as long as the borrower remains in the home and eligible, or until the term finishes. A long life could lead to one being able to withdraw more than the principal limit, especially for tenure payments, as they continue even after the line of credit is exhausted. Term payments are calculated to avoid exhausting the line of credit, but an unexpected increase in interest rates could potentially cause the loan balance to exceed the principal limit. When this happens, full payments are guaranteed as well, for the length of the term and as long as the borrower remains in the home. My reverse mortgage calculator allows users to determine the value of term and tenure payments from a reverse mortgage in addition to seeing the value of the line of credit that could be created.

Putting it All Together

In April 2016, I published an article in the *Journal of Financial Planning* that outlined my own efforts to replicate these past research findings and to more deeply compare the different options for supporting retirement spending with a HECM. I've updated that research here to maintain the same assumptions used throughout the book. The starting point includes a 10-year LIBOR Swap Rate of 2.125% and a one-month LIBOR rate of 0.4%. Assuming a 3% lender's margin rate, this leads to an expected rate of 5.125%, which translates into a principal limit factor of 50.8% for a sixty-two-year-old borrower.

In the case study I developed, I also assumed a home value of $500,000 with no remaining mortgage. At loan origination, the initial mortgage insurance premium to open the line of credit is 0.5% of the home value, or $2,500. I assume that other origination and closing costs combine for a total initial cost of $5,000 when the loan is initiated. Except for the strategy in which the line of credit is drawn down first before spending from the investment portfolio, I assume this initial cost is withdrawn from the portfolio rather than added to the loan balance. The initial effective rate for principal limit growth adds the 0.4% one-month LIBOR rate to the 3% margin and the 1.25% ongoing mortgage insurance premium, which is 4.65% initially. This variable rate will subsequently fluctuate based on simulated short-term interest rates, using my standard approach for developing Monte Carlo simulations that allows interest rates to gradually fluctuate toward their historical numbers, on average, over time.

The retiree in my study also holds $1 million in a tax-deferred investment portfolio. In order to provide a basic understanding about the impact of taxes, a marginal tax rate of 25% is applied to any portfolio distributions. Distributions from the HECM reverse mortgage do not require any tax payments. The withdrawal rate reflects post-tax inflation-adjusted spending goals as a percentage of the initial portfolio balance. For instance, a 4% withdrawal rate represents $40,000 of spending from the $1 million portfolio. The spending amount subsequently grows with the simulated inflation rate. If this distribution is taken from the portfolio, the withdrawal in real terms is \$40,000 / (1 - 0.25) = \$53,333 to cover taxes as well. If taken fully from the HECM, only \$40,000 is needed.

Within each simulation, home prices and the HECM principal limit grow randomly in response to changing short-term interest rates. In each simulation, spending is sourced from the appropriate asset based on the rules for that strategy. When a strategy calls for spending from a depleted asset (the financial portfolio or HECM), the other asset is used instead when still available. Once both assets are depleted, shortfalls below the spending goal are tabulated in order to provide a negative legacy wealth value. This is the real value of the spending shortfall without applying any investment returns or discount rates. Doing this is important to reflect the magnitude of failure with a strategy. I think this is also important as it provides a better base for comparison.

I must admit that with the past research I described, I find it confusing to compare legacy values across different strategies, because different strategies generally had retirees spending different amounts. Comparing results requires keeping track of both changes in spending and changes in legacy. I think the results I describe now are more straightforward to compare, as they are all expressed for the same spending amounts, and the inclusion of a negative legacy provides a way to incorporate shortfalls relative to a spending goal. By tracking an overall spending goal and measuring any shortfalls for the goal, the results are internally consistent and properly comparable. In previous studies, it was common to compare strategies that allowed for different levels of spending, which made it difficult to understand the meaning of different subsequent legacy wealth values.

Legacy wealth is calculated as the remaining portfolio balance plus any remaining home equity at the end of retirement. Remaining home equity is calculated as 95% of the home's value at the end of retirement less any balance due on the reverse mortgage loan. Because of the non-recourse features of the HECM program, remaining home equity cannot be negative, even if the loan balance exceeds the home's value.

Seven total retirement spending strategies will be considered, six of which involve spending from a HECM:

1. Ignore Home Equity: This is the only strategy that is not comparable with the others as it makes no use of the home equity. The strategy is only used to indicate a baseline probability of plan success when home equity is not used.

2. Home Equity as Last Resort: This strategy represents the conventional wisdom regarding home equity. It is the only home equity strategy that delays

opening a line of credit with a reverse mortgage. The investment portfolio is spent first. If and when the portfolio is depleted, a line of credit is opened with the reverse mortgage and spending needs are then met with the line of credit until it is fully used. The PLF is calculated using the current PLF table for the updated age and simulated interest rate value at the future date, assuming the same 3% lender's margin rate.

3. Use Home Equity First: This strategy opens the line of credit at the beginning of retirement, and retirement spending is covered from the line of credit first until it is fully used. This allows more time for the investment portfolio to grow before being used for withdrawals after the line of credit is depleted.

4. Sacks and Sacks Coordination Strategy: This strategy opens the line of credit at the start of retirement and withdraws from it, when available, following any years in which the investment portfolio experienced a negative market return. No efforts are made to repay the loan balance until the loan becomes due at the end of eligibility.

5. Texas Tech Coordination Strategy: This strategy is modified from the original strategy described by the Texas Tech University research team to remove the cash reserve bucket. It performs a capital needs analysis for the remaining portfolio wealth required to sustain the spending strategy over a forty-one-year time horizon. Spending is taken from the line of credit when possible—whenever the remaining portfolio balance is less than 80% of the required amount on the wealth glide path. Whenever investment wealth rises above 80% of the glide path value, any balance on the reverse mortgage is repaid as much as possible without letting wealth fall below the 80% threshold, in order to keep a lower loan balance over time and provide more growth potential for the line of credit, which was opened upon retirement.

6. Use Home Equity Last: This strategy differs from the "home equity as last resort" strategy only in that the line of credit is opened at the start of retirement. It is otherwise not used and left to grow until the investment portfolio is depleted.

7. Use Tenure Payment: This strategy uses the tenure payment option on the full value of the principal limit available. With an initial home value of $500,000, an expected rate of 5.125%, and an age sixty-two start, annual tenure payments from the line of credit are $17,247. This amount does not adjust for inflation. Any remaining spending needs are covered by the investment portfolio when possible.

Results are presented for each strategy assuming an asset allocation of 50% stocks and 50% bonds. Results are displayed for years in retirement, allowing the retirement duration to be interpreted either as the date of death or the date the borrower leaves their home and must repay the reverse mortgage loan balance.

In terms of the findings, though it should really only represent a starting point for the analysis, since it considers only one point in the distribution of outcomes, Exhibit 6.1 shows the probability that the expenditure objectives for a 4% post-tax initial spending rate can continue to be met as retirement progresses. With a 25% marginal tax rate, this would imply a gross withdrawal rate of 5.33% in the first year of retirement if distributions are taken solely from the investment portfolio.

For this exhibit, the "ignore home equity" strategy is included as a reference point, though it is not directly comparable with the others, since home equity is not used to support retirement spending. With higher expenditures to cover taxes as well, the baseline shows that the success rate for the retirement spending goal is only about 40% by the thirtieth year of retirement.

Exhibit 6.1 Probability of Success for a 4% Post-Tax Initial Withdrawal Rate, $1 million portfolio, $500,000 home value, 25% Marginal Tax Rate

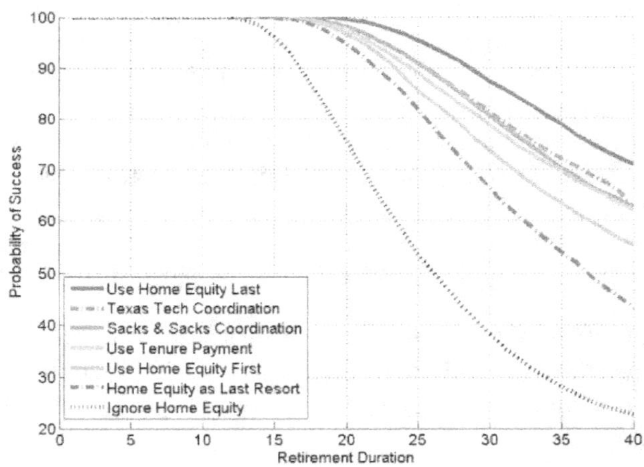

The other strategies are all comparable, because they all allow home equity to be used to meet spending goals as well. Of the six strategies that use home equity, the strategy supporting the smallest increase in success is the conventional wisdom of using home equity as a last resort and only initiating the reverse mortgage when it is first needed. This confirms the original finding from the 2012 research article by Sacks and Sacks that launched this area of inquiry.

Meanwhile, the "use home equity last" strategy provides the highest increase in success rates. Especially when interest rates are low, the line of credit will almost always be larger by the time it is needed when it is opened early and allowed to grow, than when it is opened later. Meanwhile, the benefits from the other four strategies fall somewhere in between. Success rates increase as one adjusts from using home equity first, to the tenure option, to either of the coordination strategies.

The basic understanding derived from Exhibit 6.1 is that strategies which open the line of credit early but delay its use as long as possible offer increasing success rates as more line of credit is available to be drawn from if and when it is eventually needed. This benefit from delay is sufficient to counteract the reduced sequence risk created by using the line of credit in a more coordinated way over time.

But the probability of success is not the only relevant measure for outcomes. Importantly, retirees may be concerned about the combined legacy value of their assets when using a reverse mortgage. Legacy value is defined as any remaining portfolio assets plus any remaining home equity after the reverse mortgage loan balance has been repaid. When assets were depleted (the portfolio and the entire line of credit), legacy values are counted as negative by summing the total spending shortfalls which would manifest either as reduced spending or as a need to rely on ones' heirs for additional support while alive as a form of "reverse legacy." Any taxes to be paid by heirs are not included in the numbers shown for the next three exhibits, which examine the range of legacy values. These exhibits are shown for the six strategies that incorporate home equity, so they are all comparable.

First, median wealth outcomes are mostly suggesting similar conclusions to what has been shown in previous research, though past articles have struggled to create comparable results by not accounting for negative legacy values when there are spending shortfalls. Exhibit 6.2 shows us that median legacy values remain close for the first twenty years of retirement, with spending home equity first providing the highest legacy value and spending home equity last providing the smallest. For the median outcome, the investment portfolio grows more quickly than the outstanding loan balance on the reverse mortgage, so borrowers are served best by preserving their portfolio as much as possible while spending down home equity first.

Exhibit 6.2 Median Real Legacy Value for a 4% Post-Tax Initial Withdrawal Rate, $1 million portfolio, $500,000 home value, 25% Marginal Tax Rate

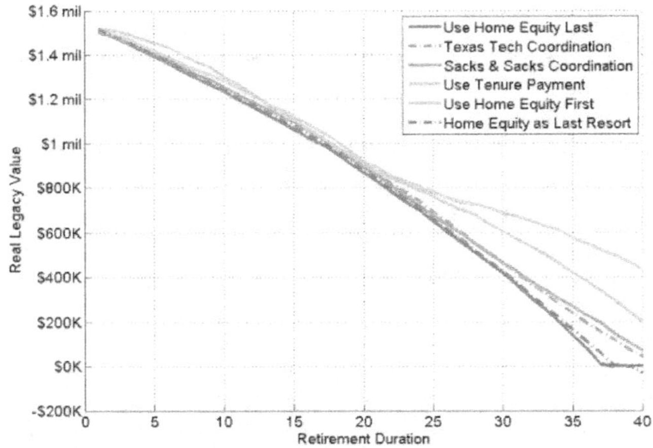

As retirement progresses, after about twenty-five years, the legacy value for the tenure payment option changes slope and starts supporting significantly more legacy. This is a combined result of the partial home equity use preserving the portfolio longer, as well as the fact that eventually tenure payments enter into the non-recourse aspect of the reverse mortgage. The tenure payments continue for as long as the retiree is in their home and meets their obligations, even if the loan balance already exceeds the full principal limit and the full value of the home. It is the only option of the six that can allow for continued spending even after the line of credit was fully utilized. When this happens, the spending has no impact on legacy, making it less costly from a legacy perspective when continuing to meet spending goals. Tenure payments become free money in the sense that there is no offset to any assets on the balance sheet thanks to the non-recourse aspect of the loan.

The other important observation to make from this exhibit is that legacy values become level at $0 when home equity is used last, as this reflects a situation in which spending is still possible from the line of credit, though the line of credit has already grown to be worth more than the home. Such spending also has no impact on legacy.

Next, Exhibit 6.3 shows the combined real legacy values at the ninetieth percentile of outcomes. These are cases when the investment portfolio performs extremely well throughout retirement. In these cases, the exhibit demonstrates that if you can count on outsized investment returns, using the line of credit more quickly can be beneficial, as the portfolio grows more quickly than the loan balance. Using home equity first, the tenure strategy, and the Sacks and Sacks coordination strategy all lean toward a quicker use of home equity than the other strategies, which support higher combined legacy values. Next is the last resort option, which is located where it is because of its ability to save on ever having to pay the upfront costs for a reverse mortgage line of credit that will not otherwise ever be used. Because markets perform so well, the insurance offered by the credit line is unused. The final two strategies open the line of credit initially but end up using it very rarely if at all, and so these provide the smallest relative advantages for legacy value.

Exhibit 6.3 90th Percentile Real Legacy Value for a 4% Post-Tax Initial Withdrawal Rate, $1 million portfolio, $500,000 home value, 25% Marginal Tax Rate

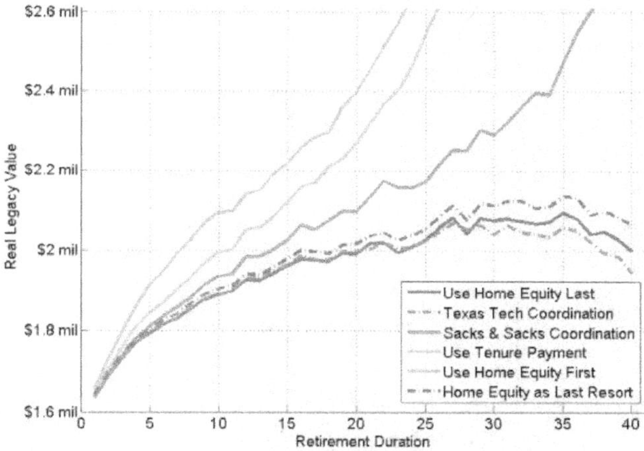

Finally, while Exhibit 6.3 shows what happens when markets perform extremely well, Exhibit 6.4 shows results for the tenth percentile of outcomes when market performance is poor. These are the bad luck cases for market returns and sequence risk, in which planning generally focuses on providing a workable solution. In such cases, legacy values reach $0 by about twenty-five years into retirement. Spending down home equity first becomes the riskiest strategy, as the delay in having to start tapping the portfolio hasn't sufficiently helped if financial markets are significantly down a few years into retirement. Once retirements last longer, eventually, spending home equity last (after opening the line of credit early) does the best to continue supporting spending even after financial assets are depleted. In poor market environments, the line of credit growth can be expected to exceed market returns. For some years, the chance of benefitting from a line of credit which exceeds the home value is higher, and then helps slow the eventual portfolio shortfalls that arise once both retirement resources have been fully depleted. The tenure option also provides some spending support to reduce the size of shortfalls even after both resources are depleted, which happens at the tenth percentile of outcomes. This continued cash flow explains the change in direction for the legacy values after depletion, which is why the tenure option looks second best after forty years of retirement.

Exhibit 6.4 10th Percentile Real Legacy Value for a 4% Post-Tax Initial Withdrawal Rate, $1 million portfolio, $500,000 home value, 25% Marginal Tax Rate

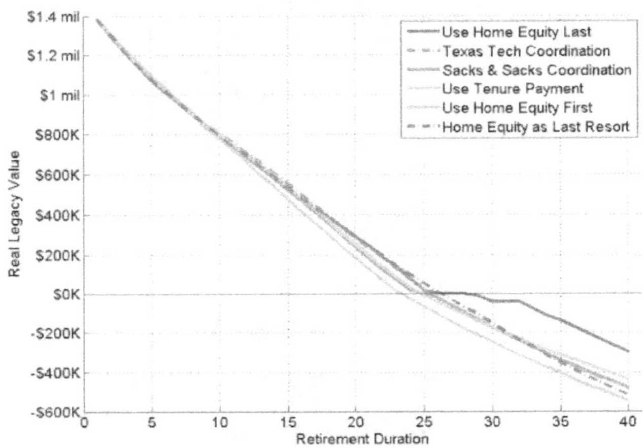

As you can see, strategies that spend the home equity more quickly increase the overall risk for the retirement plan. More upside potential is generated by delaying the need to take distributions from investments, but more downside risk is created because the home equity is used quickly without necessarily being compensated by sufficiently high market returns.

Meanwhile, opening the line of credit at the start of retirement and then delaying its use until the portfolio is depleted creates the most downside protection for the retirement income plan. This strategy allows the line of credit to grow for longer, perhaps surpassing the home's value before it is used. It provides a bigger base to continue retirement spending after the portfolio is depleted. Using home equity last reduces upside potential because when markets are strong, the portfolio will grow faster than the loan balance.

Frequently, this line of credit growth opportunity serves a stronger role than the benefits from mitigating sequence risk through the use of coordinated strategies. Nonetheless, use of tenure payments or one of the coordinated strategies can also be justified as providing a middle ground, which balances the upside potential of using home equity first and the downside protection of using home equity last.

These coordinated strategies can occasionally provide the best outcomes for legacy in some simulated cases when they best balance the tradeoff between using home equity soon to provide relief for the portfolio, and delaying home equity use so the available line of credit is larger. It is important to note that strategies that open a line of credit and leave it unused run counter to the objectives of lenders and the government's mortgage insurance fund. Though they still exist today, one day these opportunities may become more limited. Ultimately, the tenure option looks to be a good compromise for the interests of all parties involved.

Further Reading

Pfau, Wade D. 2016. "Incorporating Home Equity into a Retirement Income Strategy." *Journal of Financial Planning* 29 (4): 41-49.

Pfeiffer, Shaun, C. Angus Schaal, and John Salter. 2014. "HECM Reverse Mortgages: Now or Last Resort?" *Journal of Financial Planning* 27 (5): 44–51.

Pfeiffer, Shaun, John R. Salter, and Harold R. Evensky. 2013. "Increasing the Sustainable Withdrawal Rate Using the Standby Reverse Mortgage." *Journal of Financial Planning* 26 (12): 55-62.

Sacks, Barry H., and Stephen R. Sacks. 2012. "Reversing the Conventional Wisdom: Using Home Equity to Supplement Retirement Income." *Journal of Financial Planning* 25 (2): 43-52.

Salter, John R., Shaun A. Pfeiffer, and Harold R. Evensky. 2012. "Standby Reverse Mortgages: A Risk Management Tool for Retirement Distributions." *Journal of Financial Planning* 25 (8): 40-48.

Wagner, Gerald C. 2013. "The 6.0 Percent Rule." *Journal of Financial Planning* 26 (12): 46-59.

CHAPTER 7: PORTFOLIO COORDINATION FOR RETIREMENT HOUSING

Coordinating housing-related issues with the investment portfolio and a reverse mortgage can be a critical step in a structurally sound retirement plan. For retirees carrying a traditional mortgage into retirement, the two best options are to use a HECM to pay off the existing mortgage and then not worry about repaying the loan balance until it becomes due, or to use the HECM to pay off an existing mortgage and then continue making voluntary payments to reduce the size of the loan balance throughout retirement.

Other relevant HECM uses include funding home renovations with the HECM to better allow for aging in place. The point is simply that the HECM can be used as a source of funds for renovations. This strategy may allow homeowners to remain in their homes longer than would otherwise be possible, and it could also provide a way to maintain the value of the home and avoid deterioration of the property. The strategy can also reduce the need to move to a more institutionalized setting—or at least delay this move—later in retirement. Home renovations made with a reverse mortgage could include other ideas mentioned, such as adding a walk-in bathing facility on the first floor of the home or creating a ramp entrance to the home.

A final matter to consider is how to use the HECM for Purchase program to purchase a new home in retirement. Some of the strategies discussed in this chapter provide an allowance within the HECM rules that the borrower may take more than 60% of the initial principal limit during the first year of the loan. It is important to keep in mind whether the borrower may have other alternative resources available to keep under the 60% borrowing limit that triggers the initial mortgage insurance premium to rise from 0.5% of the home's value to 2.5% of the home's value. For a $500,000 home, that's a $10,000 difference in costs. You may wish to consider whether it is possible to draw from other resources if necessary to avoid borrowing more than 60% of the principal limit and facing the 2.5% insurance premium.

Strategies for Carrying a Mortgage Into Retirement

More Americans are now entering into their retirements while still carrying a mortgage. In 2014, the Consumer Finance Protection Bureau reported that the percentage of those aged sixty-five and older with a mortgage rose from 22% in 2001 to 30% in 2011. This represented a rise from 3.8 million to 6.1 million

Americans. Among individuals over seventy-five, those who still had mortgages rose from 8.4% to 21.2%.

Mortgage debt in retirement is an additional challenge. For retirement distributions, fixed payments related to paying off debt create a strain for retirees due to the heightened withdrawal needs triggering greater exposure to sequence of returns risk. Exposure rises because the debt payments are fixed and require greater distributions than otherwise, so if there is a market decline early in retirement, the portfolio is strained as an even greater percentage of what is left in the portfolio must be taken in order to meet these fixed expenses.

When using a reverse mortgage primarily as a way to pay off an existing mortgage, the general idea is that doing so will create more flexibility for distribution needs from the investment portfolio by removing a fixed expense from household budgeting. During pre-retirement, it is common to pay off the mortgage more slowly in hopes that investment returns will outpace the borrowing costs on the mortgage.

Those with sufficient risk tolerance may wish to continue with this approach post-retirement, but the risk of keeping the mortgage increases due to the heightened sequence risk caused by distributions that amplifies the effects of investment volatility. In addition, a changing tax situation with the loss of wages and the dwindling mortgage balance in retirement could mean losing potential tax deductions for mortgage interest, which would result in saving less on taxes.

By paying off the existing mortgage with a reverse mortgage, you could voluntarily continue making the same monthly payments on the loan balance of the reverse mortgage to reduce it and increase the growing credit line amount for future use. But this is unnecessary and probably less than ideal, as these repayments could also be strategically made when markets are performing well and then stopped when it would be necessary to sell assets at a loss to make payments. With a traditional mortgage, stopping payments in this way is not allowed and can trigger foreclosure.

The benefit of replacing a mortgage with a reverse mortgage, then, is the reduced exposure to sequence risk. However, it is also important to note that the growth rate on the reverse mortgage loan balance could exceed the interest rate on the pre-existing mortgage, especially if interest rates rise from their current levels. You would have to balance the tradeoffs between the increased flexibility and reduced cash flows to be supported earlier in retirement against the possibility that the final legacy value for assets could be hurt if the HECM loan balance is not repaid for many years.

Whether the final legacy increases or decreases when using a reverse mortgage in this way also depends on the performance of the investment portfolio, which requires lower distributions, leaving assets with more time in the market.

We can analyze this problem with the same Monte Carlo simulation framework used to consider coordinated spending strategies in the previous chapter. For a retiree carrying a traditional mortgage into retirement, the question becomes what to do with it. Let's consider four potential scenarios:

1. Pay off mortgage at retirement with financial assets; only use HECM as last resort if and when assets are depleted

2. Keep mortgage into retirement, making the required ongoing payments until the mortgage has been fully paid off; only use HECM as last resort if and when assets are depleted;

3. Use HECM to pay off mortgage balance; use remaining line of credit last to cover spending if portfolio is depleted

4. Keep mortgage into retirement, making the required ongoing payments until the mortgage has been fully paid off; open the HECM line of credit after the mortgage has been paid off and use it last

These possibilities can provide a sense about how keeping a mortgage compares with using a HECM to cover the mortgage. For this example, a sixty-five-year-old couple is entering into retirement. Twenty years ago, the couple purchased a $300,000 home with a 20% down payment, using a 7.5% fixed thirty-year mortgage for the rest of the home price. Mortgage rates have declined since then, and they have not refinanced to keep the example at a more basic level. Refinancing would not change the results by too much. For this mortgage, their annual payments are $20,321. And with ten years left on the mortgage, their remaining mortgage balance today is $139,485. Over the past twenty years, their home has appreciated at an average rate of 3%. It is worth $541,833 today.

We keep the same assumptions as before for the HECM: the 10-year LIBOR swap rate is 2.125%, and the lender's margin is 3%. For a sixty-five-year old, this translates into an initial PLF of 52.6%, with the expected rate of 5.125%. Upfront costs include 0.5% of the home value for the MIP plus another $2,500, adjusting for inflation if the reverse mortgage is opened at some point in the future. Whenever a reverse mortgage is initiated, I assume the upfront costs will be financed within the loan.

I do check to keep HECM mortgage payment below the 60% threshold, which triggers a higher upfront MIP. This doesn't happen in the scenario since the mortgage balance is less than 60% of the initial principal limit. The principal limit is 52.6% of $541,833, or $285,004. Sixty percent of this value is $171,002, which is more than sufficient to cover the $139,485 mortgage balance and upfront costs.

Again, I assume that retirement date financial assets consist of $1 million in a tax-deferred retirement account, and the marginal tax rate is 25%. The investment portfolio uses a 50/50 asset allocation for stocks and bonds. Finally, the spending goal for retirement expenses net of any taxes or required mortgage payments is an inflation-adjusted $40,000.

Exhibit 7.1 shows the results for this example, in terms of the ongoing probability of success throughout retirement. The worst outcome occurs by carrying the reverse mortgage into retirement and using a HECM only as a last resort. This strategy creates the most sequence risk, since ongoing distribution obligations remain higher to cover mortgage payments as well, leading to a larger negative impact on the retirement plan after a market decline early in retirement. Next, small improvements in the success probability rise if the mortgage is simply paid off with investment assets at the start of retirement. Because this example starts with $1 million at the retirement date, it does not incorporate pre-retirement sequence risk. Paying the mortgage upfront reduces the risk that market losses will stress the ability to make ongoing payments.

Exhibit 7.1 Probability of Success for a 4% Post-Tax Initial Withdrawal Rate, $1 million portfolio, $541,833 home value, 25% Marginal Tax Rate

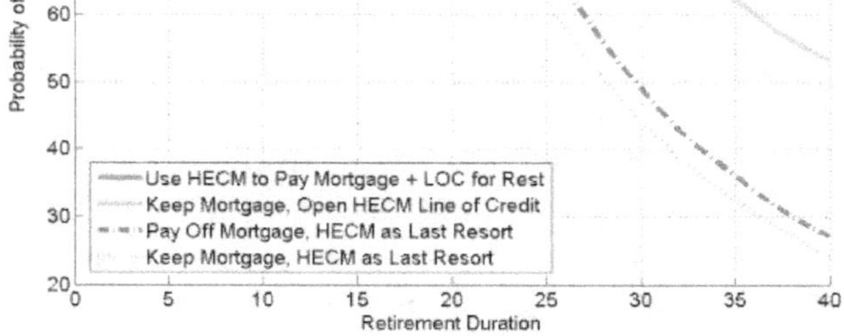

Moving on to higher success rates, the next strategy is to keep the mortgage, but open a line of credit ten years later after the mortgage is repaid, for later

use if the portfolio becomes depleted. The purpose for including this strategy is to provide a baseline comparison for the strategy which shows the largest increase in success rates: open a HECM and use the proceeds to pay off the existing mortgage, and then use any remaining amount to cover expenses if the portfolio depletes.

Using a HECM to pay off the mortgage allows the success rate to be 90% after thirty years of retirement, whereas the success rate cannot rise above 50% if the HECM is only opened later as a last resort. This is a remarkable difference in outcomes which suggests that the HECM option should be considered carefully for those who are entering into their retirements while still carrying a traditional mortgage on their home.

HECM for Purchase

The other alternative within this category of HECM use is the HECM for Purchase program, which was started in 2009 as a way to use a reverse mortgage to purchase a new home. The government saw enough people using a costlier and more complicated two-step process—first obtaining a traditional mortgage to purchase the home and then using a reverse mortgage to pay off that mortgage—that it sought to simplify the process and costs.

With an example of a sixty-two-year-old, a 5.125% expected rate, and a principal limit factor of 50.8%, the HECM for Purchase could cover this portion of the home's cost. The other 49.2% would need to be financed from other assets, such as selling the previous primary residence. The remaining amount not covered by the HECM cannot be financed using other debt. Also, to keep the initial mortgage insurance premium down, the borrower would only want to tap 60% of the initial principal limit—30.48% of the home's value—and finance the other 69.52% through other resources. Those resources could be paid back after one year has passed, so the 49.2% number would effectively still apply then. After that point, the new home is owned with a debt that does not need to be repaid until the borrower leaves the home or is otherwise no longer eligible for the loan.

In terms of coordinating the use of debt for housing, not having to make a monthly mortgage payment reduces the household's fixed costs and provides potential relief for the need to spend down investments. The HECM for Purchase option could be analyzed relative to paying outright for the home with other assets, or by potentially opening a fifteen-year mortgage, if this is still feasible.

Should the borrower live in the home long enough, the loan balance may grow to exceed the value of the home, setting the no-recourse aspect of the loan into motion. In this situation, one could interpret the HECM for Purchase program as a way to provide housing services as long as the borrower remains eligible for an upfront cost of 49.2% of the home's value.

Should the borrower leave the home while the loan balance is still less than the home value, the home could be sold with any remaining equity still available to the borrower after the loan is repaid.

The HECM for Purchase program could be used to either downsize or upsize a retirement home. For those downsizing, the HECM for Purchase could free up more assets from the sale of the previous home to be used for other purposes. For those upsizing with the financial resources to manage this sustainably and *responsibly,* the HECM for Purchase could allow for a more expensive home—especially considering that obtaining a traditional mortgage may become increasingly difficult after retirement.

Suppose the retiree wants to move from a $300,000 home to a $600,000 home. If the PLF is over 50%, the proceeds from selling the previous home combined with the credit available through the HECM for Purchase would cover the cost of the new home. Of course, the borrower may want to avoid the 2.5% initial mortgage insurance premium and must otherwise manage upfront mortgage costs, but this is the basic process for upsizing without otherwise tapping into investments or taking out a new traditional mortgage.

Further Reading

Consumer Finance Protection Bureau. 2014. Snapshot of Older Consumers and Mortgage Debt. [Link]

CHAPTER 8: THE TENURE PAYMENT AS AN ANNUITY ALTERNATIVE

When comparing different strategies for coordinating home equity with portfolio distributions to generate retirement income, the tenure option fairs well and looks to be an appealing option. As a way to fund retirement efficiency improvements, using the tenure payment option from the line of credit as an alternative to purchasing an income annuity is worth exploring further. The tenure option annuitizes home equity as an alternative to annuitizing financial assets. If you are considering income annuities as you approach retirement, what could be a more effective way to building an income stream: purchasing an income annuity, or using a tenure payment option on a reverse mortgage? A tenure payment behaves similar to an income annuity, though they are not the same.

First, to be clear, a tenure payment does not necessarily provide a guaranteed monthly cash flow for life as an income annuity would. Guaranteed cash flow continues only as long as the borrower remains eligible by staying in the home and meeting homeowner obligations. Moving away from the home for more than a year would end the payments. While a non-borrowing spouse may remain in the home if the borrower is no longer eligible, tenure payments would stop once the borrower has become ineligible. Only when both spouses are eligible would the tenure payment behave like a joint-life annuity.

Another difference is that no lump-sum payment (other than any upfront reverse mortgage costs) must be given up from the portfolio to initiate the tenure payments. Each tenure payment is taken from the line of credit and moved to the loan balance. In the event that the retiree dies early, the loan balance may be substantially less than an annuity premium would have been. Conceptually, the tenure payment behaves more closely to an income annuity with a cash refund provision, in terms of whether any assets would be available at the end of the contracted period. Still, there was no upfront lump sum to initiate these payments with the tenure option. This is an important distinction.

The tenure payment also does not provide mortality credits in a conventional sense. Its pricing is based on an assumption that the borrower or borrowers live to age 100. Despite the lack of traditional mortality credits, tenure payments provide a degree of longevity protection, assuming the borrower remains eligible. Cash flow received from the line of credit through the tenure payment can exceed the value of the principal limit and can even exceed the value of the home. Once this happens, the non-recourse aspects of the loan provide spending power without a tradeoff to legacy in a way philosophically similar to an income annuity. That non-recourse aspect could be interpreted as a type of "mortality credit."

A final difference is that the formulas to calculate tenure payout rates and income annuity payout rates are different. As discussed before, the tenure payout rate depends on the 10-year LIBOR swap rate plus a lender's margin and mortgage insurance premium rate of 1.25%. It also depends on an assumed time horizon or "life expectancy" of age 100. It does not vary by gender or whether payments are for one or two eligible borrowers.

Meanwhile, an income annuity depends on actual mortality data for the age and gender of the individual or couple, as well as on a lower interest rate that may be a bit higher than a 10-year LIBOR swap rate, but that doesn't include a lender's margin or mortgage insurance premium.

For the tenure payment, the higher interest rate supports higher payments than an income annuity. But the assumption that "life expectancy" is age 100 supports lower payments, relative to the income annuity. However, the higher interest rate assumption should more than counterbalance the age 100 assumption in most cases, so the tenure payments imply a larger payout rate than an income annuity.

For example, as I write, the 10-year LIBOR swap rate is about 2.1%. For a tenure payment to a sixty-five-year-old with a lender's margin of 3%, the payout rate for the tenure payment option is 7.1%. We can compare this rate to annuity quotes with cash refunds offered through ImmediateAnnuities.com for sixty-five-year-olds. The payout is 6.15% for a single male, 6.07% for a female, and 5.61% for couples. Women and couples especially benefit from the tenure payment, as it does not penalize them for their longer relative life expectancies.

Another interesting aspect to consider for tenure payments is that, surprisingly, the monthly tenure payment amount for a given home value is actually higher when interest rates are low. Naturally, higher interest rates allow for a higher payout rate from the principal limit amount as just discussed. This is documented at the top of Exhibit 8.1 for expected rates between 5% and 10%, in the case of a sixty-five-year-old borrower with a $300,000 home. The payout rate from the principal limit increases from 7.01% when the expected rate is 5%, to 11.37% when the expected rate is 10%. However, the initial principal limit that the payout rate is applied to decreases as rates rise, creating a much stronger counter-effect. For a sixty-five-year-old borrower, an expected rate of 5% supports a principal limit factor of 54.2%. The principal limit factor falls to 14.8% when the expected rate is 10%.

Exhibit 8.1 The Relationship between Expected Rates and Tenure Payments, $300,000 home value, sixty-five-year old borrower

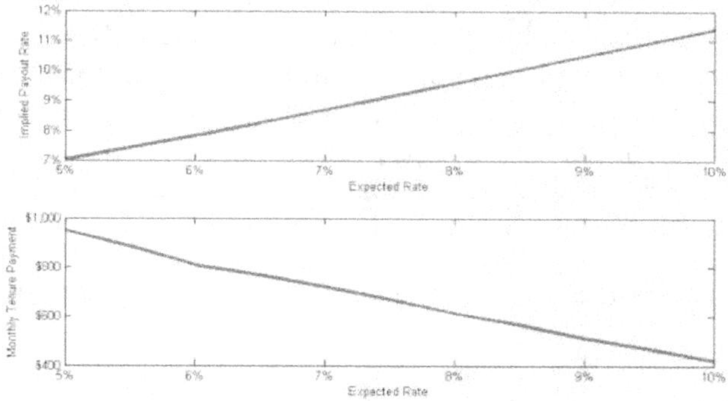

The combined impact of the higher payout rate applied to a smaller principal limit is shown in the bottom of the figure. The monthly available tenure payment decreases as interest rates rise. It was $950 per month with a 5% expected rate, falling to just $421 per month with a 10% expected rate. The surprising implication is that tenure payments will represent a higher percentage of the home's value when interest rates are low. With income annuities, a given lump-sum premium would support a larger monthly payment when interest rates are higher. Of course, the principal limit not the home value would provide an equivalent amount to annuitize, but the interesting point is that low interest rates allow for more annuitized spending for a household with a given ratio of home value to portfolio size.

About whether to choose tenure payments or income annuities, Exhibit 8.2 provides circumstances which would favor one or the other. First, as noted, couples and single females would experience lower payout rates from income annuities, as their pricing considers their increased longevity relative to single males. Single males can receive the highest relative payout rates from income annuities and would have a stronger reason to consider them, relatively speaking. Second, tenure payments make more sense for those planning to remain in their homes, as they have more opportunity to spread out any upfront costs and potentially receive a windfall from the non-recourse aspect of tenure payments. For those likely to move, or who otherwise do not live in an eligible home, income annuities have an edge.

Next, for those with less risk aversion, tenure payments are worth considering as a way to obtain more guaranteed cash flows without having to take dollars out of the stock market. For income annuities, I suggest treating the annuitized assets as part of your bond holdings, but in practice this can be difficult because the remaining investment portfolio would become more stock-heavy and volatile.

In practice, real-world considerations will probably mean partial annuitization will also reduce stock holdings for most retirees, but the full portfolio and original asset allocation can remain intact more easily with the tenure payment option. Finally, as noted, in a low-interest-rate environment, a given home value can support a higher tenure payment than otherwise. This gives tenure payments an edge to provide more spending power for a given home value to financial portfolio ratio, relative to income annuities.

Exhibit 8.2 Circumstances Favoring Tenure Payments or Income Annuities

Tenure Payment	Income Annuity
Couples	Single Male
Plan to remain in eligible home	Likely to Move; Live in ineligible home
Less risk averse	More risk averse
Shorter life expectancy	Longer life expectancy
Low-interest-rate environment	High-interest-rate environment

Tenure payments have many favorable characteristics. A tenure payment allows for an annuitized spending stream generated by home equity, subject to the caveat that it may not last for life if the borrower moves or cannot maintain the home. It does not require assets to be extracted as a large lump-sum annuity premium.

For individuals uncomfortable with increasing their stock allocation for remaining assets after partial annuitization, the tenure payment option would allow more assets to remain in the stock market and focused on growth. It offers a higher payout rate, which in turn would require more annuitization to receive the same amount of spending as the tenure payments. The tenure payments are not added to adjustable gross income, whereas the annuity income would be subject to taxes when initiated from either tax-deferred or taxable resources.

Simulating Tenure Payment and Income Annuity Options

In terms of research providing simulations to quantify these comparisons, Joe Tomlinson, a financial planner in Maine, initiated work on comparing reverse mortgage options and income annuities with a column he wrote for *Advisor Perspectives* in April 2015. He followed that column up with more detailed joint research with John Salter and Shaun Pfeiffer for an article published in the Spring 2016 issue of the *Journal of Personal Finance.* Two of the options compared are relevant for our discussion: initiating tenure payments with a reverse mortgage, and purchasing enough income annuity to obtain the same payments as the tenure option could provide while also opening a line of credit on the reverse mortgage and only using it if needed later in life.

Tomlinson, Salter, and Pfeiffer found that longevity-protected cash flows can enhance retirement spending, even compared to a strategy of opening a line of credit and delaying its use. The researchers further found evidence that using home equity can provide greater spending support than carving out a portion of assets to purchase an income annuity. They considered scenarios when interest rates remain low and when interest rates rise shortly after retirement begins, after the reverse mortgage and income annuity decisions have already been made.

Compared to buying an income annuity and opening a line of credit, the tenure payment option supports more spending on average as well as a larger average legacy. These outcomes also hold if interest rates subsequently rise, though the differences are smaller as the line of credit is able to grow faster and support more spending later in the case that an income annuity is combined with opening a line of credit. The tenure payment option allows more dollars to remain in the stock market, which helps, on average.

On the downside, the income annuity strategy provided more income at the fifth percentile of the distribution, especially if interest rates rise in the future. This finding is contingent upon opening the line of credit at the start of retirement when also annuitizing, and then delaying the line of credit use until the portfolio is depleted.

The research approach used by Tomlinson's team differs a bit from my usual approach. They track the amount of spending that could be generated by different strategies, while I tend to focus on how well different strategies are able to meet a fixed spending objective and what sorts of shortfalls may arise in the effort to meet that spending objective. I have created an analysis along these lines and can confirm their general findings that the tenure option can provide a potentially attractive alternative to partial annuitization.

Consider a scenario similar to the one we used to compare different portfolio coordination strategies in chapter six. A couple reaches age sixty-five with a $500,000 home and $1 million in tax-deferred retirement plans. In addition to income from Social Security and other sources, they would like to fund another $40,000 from their assets in inflation-adjusted and after-tax terms. They are in the 25% marginal tax bracket (this is the tax rate they pay on distributions from their investment assets). To meet their $40,000 spending objective, they need to withdraw enough to also cover taxes. They would need $53,333 from their retirement plan to have $40,000 left after taxes. But since reverse mortgage distributions are not taxable income, a $40,000 distribution would cover their need.

I consider a HECM when the 10-year LIBOR swap rate is 2.125% and with a margin rate of 3%. This leads to a PLF of 52.6%, and a principal limit of $263,000. With upfront costs totaling $5,000 paid from their investments, the available tenure payment for this HECM loan is $18,698. For income annuities, using ImmediateAnnuities.com, they find that a joint-life annuity with fixed lifetime payments and a cash refund provision has a payout rate of 5.54%. A life-only version has a payout of 5.65%, but the cash refund provision makes the income more comparable to how the legacy cost of tenure payments would be determined, with each tenure payment added to the loan balance as it happens. The couple is also comfortable with an asset allocation of 50% stocks and 50% bonds for their investment portfolio.

I consider four scenarios for using reverse mortgages and income annuities as part of the retirement income plan:

1. Investments-only: The couple does not purchase an income annuity and they only open a reverse mortgage as a last resort option in the event that their portfolio is depleted.

2. Tenure payment: The couple uses the tenure payment for a HECM, which provides $18,698 annually without inflation adjustments. This represents 7.1% of the principal limit. Any remaining distributions needed to meet their spending objectives are taken from their investment portfolio.

3. Income Annuity Purchased Proportionately from Investments: The couple takes $263,000 (the equivalent principal amount) from their retirement account and purchases a joint-life income annuity with a payout rate of 5.54%. This supports $14,570 of annual income before taxes, or $10,928 after taxes are paid. For assets remaining in their investment portfolio, they maintain an allocation of 50% stocks and 50% bonds. A HECM line of credit is only opened as a last resort option later in retirement if the portfolio is depleted.

4. Income Annuity Purchased as Bond Alternative: The couple takes $263,000 from their retirement account and purchases a joint-life income annuity. This is the same as the previous scenario. The difference is that this purchase is made with only bonds, so the stock allocation for the remaining investment portfolio increases to keep the same amount of stocks as before. The new asset allocation for remaining investments is 67% stocks and 33% bonds. A HECM line of credit is only opened as a last resort option later in retirement if the portfolio is depleted.

The next exhibits provide the results for these four strategies, beginning with the probability of success in Exhibit 8.3. Because the withdrawal rate from the portfolio needed to generate $40,000 after tax is 5.33%, and the initial payout rate from the income annuity is 5.54%, the income annuity does not have much impact on the probability of success if the same asset allocation is maintained after annuitization. The annuity slightly reduces portfolio withdrawal needs at the start of retirement, but inflation will erode this benefit quickly and then portfolio withdrawals eventually must be greater. Nonetheless, the probability of success for option three (partial annuitization with the same asset allocation) closely matches that of the no income annuity case. Both cases open a reverse mortgage only as a last resort option, which I have shown before is the worst possible way to use home equity to support retirement spending.

Exhibit 8.3 Probability of Success for a 4% Post-Tax Initial Withdrawal Rate, $1 million portfolio, $500,000 home value, 25% Marginal Tax Rate

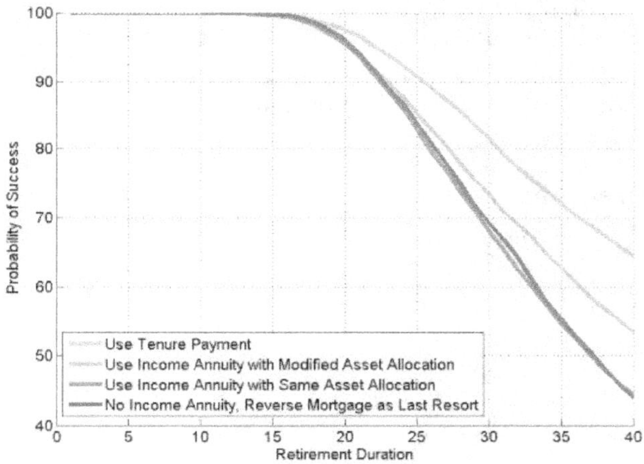

After thirty years, the income annuity with a modified asset allocation provides about a 73% chance of success, compared to about 68% for the previously described strategies. Probability of success is improved when an income annuity is purchased using bonds. Income annuities provide similar investment returns as bonds, and after life expectancy they provide a unique source of additional returns in the form of mortality credits. These mortality credits explain the improved performance when the amount of stocks held is allowed to remain the same at retirement.

Exhibit 8.3 also reveals that the tenure payment option is the big winner among these choices. It consistently supports a higher probability of success than the income annuity by leaving more in the investment portfolio, by supporting spending without adding to adjusted gross income, and by reducing portfolio distributions and sequence of returns risk. With the tenure payment, the probability of success is about 80% after thirty years.

In Exhibit 8.4, we track median inflation-adjusted legacy wealth over time. Legacy wealth consists of remaining investment assets, remaining home equity after loan repayment, and any cash refund on the income annuity in the event of an early death. The tenure payment option consistently helps support the largest legacy value of assets at the median, and the gap for its improvement widens after about twenty years of retirement. At this point, the loan balance surpasses the home value, so subsequent payments continue to be received without any negative offset to legacy. The tenure payments continue as long as the retiree is in their home and meets his obligations, even if the loan balance already exceeds the full principal limit and the full value of the home.

The tenure payment option provides longevity protection subject to the borrower remaining in the home and eligible, and it allows more assets to remain invested in the portfolio. It also reduces the demand on portfolio distributions, which mitigates sequence risk. At least at the median, the tenure payment offers potentially attractive outcomes for retirees relative to partially annuitizing a similar set of assets.

Exhibit 8.4 Median Real Legacy Value for a 4% Post-Tax Initial Withdrawal Rate, $1 million portfolio, $500,000 home value, 25% Marginal Tax Rate

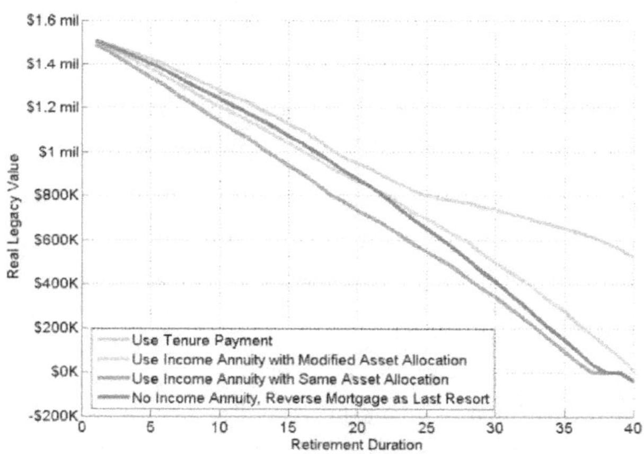

The next two sets of lines in the exhibit reflect a case with no income annuity and no tenure payment, and a case where an income annuity is purchased with assets taken from the bond portion of the portfolio (modified asset allocation). Both options use a reverse mortgage only as a last resort. The pattern seen with these two lines reflects patterns I have shown elsewhere, as the no annuity case supports a slightly larger legacy in the short-term (with the difference being that the cash refund provision on the income annuity assumes an investment return of 0% that lags behind actual portfolio returns in the median), but a larger legacy in the long-term as mortality credits start to provide a unique source of additional returns beyond what could be received from the investment portfolio. Mortality credits slow portfolio depletion, but we must recognize that when taxes are considered, the 5.33% withdrawal rate needed to meet the post-tax spending objective is rather aggressive and risky. Though the income annuity improves the situation, it is a challenge to keep pace with this aggressive spending goal.

The worst outcome in this exhibit is the partial annuitization case when the amount of stocks held is reduced because the asset allocation remains the same after partial annuitization. In the median outcome, holding less in stocks and missing the realized upside hurts legacy outcomes.

Exhibit 8.5 provides outcomes at the ninetieth percentile when markets perform exceptionally well. Again, the tenure payment option consistently comes out ahead of the other strategies. It keeps more invested in the markets at a time they do well, and it provides more relief for portfolio withdrawals, which allows more assets to remain in the portfolio and to grow.

The next line in the exhibit is partial annuitization with the modified asset allocation reflecting that the annuitized assets are taken from bonds. This type of allocation allows for a higher subsequent stock allocation. The market gains at the ninetieth percentile allow this strategy to shine. The no income annuity option falls next in the ranking of outcomes, since this strategy also allows more to remain in the market at a time markets did well. Finally, the income annuity option with the same asset allocation removes the most growth potential for the portfolio and leaves the relative smallest amount of legacy at the ninetieth percentile of the distribution.

Exhibit 8.5 90th Percentile Real Legacy Value for a 4% Post-Tax Initial Withdrawal Rate, $1 million portfolio, $500,000 home value, 25% Marginal Tax Rate

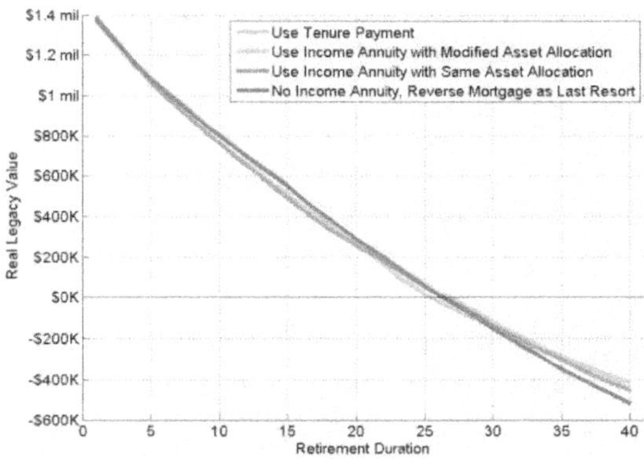

Finally, while Exhibit 8.4 shows what happened when markets perform extremely well, Exhibit 8.6 shows results for the tenth percentile of outcomes when market performance is poor. These are the bad luck cases for market returns and sequence risk, in which planning generally focuses on providing a workable solution.

Exhibit 8.6 10th Percentile Real Legacy Value for a 4% Post-Tax Initial Withdrawal Rate, $1 million portfolio, $500,000 home value, 25% Marginal Tax Rate

What we find is that there is very little difference in outcomes for any of the strategies shown in Exhibit 8.6. The investment portfolio is depleted rapidly before credit lines have an opportunity to grow. The tenure and income annuity options support some spending after portfolio depletion, which changes the slope for these legacy lines, but the effect is fairly small, as observable in the diagram. Simply put, the withdrawal strategy is too aggressive for cases in which market returns do not cooperate during retirement.

Further Reading

Tomlinson, Joseph. 2015. "New Research: Reverse Mortgages, SPIAs and Retirement Income." *Advisor Perspectives* (April 14). [Link]

Tomlinson, Joseph, Shaun Pfeiffer, and John Salter. 2016. "Reverse Mortgages, Annuities, and Investments: Sorting Out the Options to Generate Sustainable Retirement Income." *Journal of Personal Finance* 15 (1): 27-36.

CHAPTER 9: PROTECTING THE HOME VALUE

The final use for a reverse mortgage is to preserve the line of credit as an insurance policy against a variety of retirement risks. Preserving credit as insurance involves setting up a HECM reverse mortgage as early as possible and then leaving it unused until needed. The upfront costs for the reverse mortgage could be treated as an insurance premium that may never need to be used if everything else goes well in retirement. However, a variety of potential pitfalls face retirees, and implementing a reverse mortgage earlier in retirement could support a sizeable pool of contingency assets.

I have already discussed one aspect of this insurance protection in chapter six, in which a line of credit is opened and then only used to support retirement spending in the event of portfolio depletion. In this regard, the insurance provided by the HECM is against market losses that risk the ability to meet retirement portfolio distribution goals. I have shown that the strategy to open a reverse mortgage early and then only spend from it as a last resort provides the most downside protection for retirees in terms of enhancing retirement success rates and preserving the legacy value of assets in bad market environments.

Another aspect of the insurance that could be provided by a HECM line of credit is to treat it as a large contingency fund to help meet unplanned expenses. For example, a reverse mortgage could also help as part of a divorce settlement. In this scenario, the reverse mortgage could allow one ex-spouse to stay in the home, with the reverse mortgage used to pay a necessary portion of the home's equity to the other ex-spouse. Alternatively, the home could be sold with the proceeds split, and then each of the ex-spouses could use their half of the home equity with a HECM for Purchase to obtain a similarly valued home as the original. The line of credit could also be used to support in-home care or other health expenses to avoid or delay institutional living in the face of long-term care needs.

The focus of this chapter is a final insurance aspect that requires a bit more explanation: using the HECM as a way to protect the value of your home. With the current HECM rules, those living in their homes long enough could reap a large windfall when the line of credit exceeds the home's value. This potential windfall is amplified by today's low interest rates. Even if the value of the home declines, the line of credit will continue to grow without regard for the home's subsequent value.

Combining this with the fact that a HECM is a non-recourse loan means the HECM provides a valuable hedging property for home prices. What is the specific probability that the value of a standby line of credit will grow to exceed the home value? I have sought to answer this by simulating future home prices and future one-month LIBOR rates that will guide the growth of the line of credit. With each of these values projected over time, we can determine how frequently a line of credit may exceed the value of the home across a large number of simulated futures.

For this example, I assume the borrowers are sixty-two years old, the 10-year LIBOR swap rate is 2.125%, the current one-month LIBOR rate is 0.4%, the lender's margin is 3%, and upfront costs will be financed from the investment portfolio. This combination results in an expected rate of 5.125% and a principal limit factor of 50.8%.

The initial effective rate is 4.65% (0.4% LIBOR, 3% lender's margin, and 1.25% mortgage insurance premium). If interest rates never rose, it would take far too long for a 1.65% spread in the growth rate (4.65% less 3% for home values) to allow the line of credit, which is initially 50.8% of the home value, to grow and surpass the home value. With fixed growth rates, the line of credit would not exceed the home value until the borrower is 109 years old. But, if we forecast one-month LIBOR rates to gradually increase in the future, the increased variable rates for the HECM line of credit make the odds quite attractive for seeing the line of credit eventually exceed the home price. As an example to help with the intuition, if one-month LIBOR rates immediately and permanently increased by 1%, the breakeven age falls from 109 to ninety. An immediate increase of 2%, which would still leave short-term interest rates below historical averages, would further reduce the breakeven age to eighty-two.

Exhibit 9.1 shows the probabilities by age that the HECM line of credit has grown to exceed the home's value for a sixty-two-year-old borrower. With these simulations, there is a 50% chance by age eighty-one that the line of credit has exceeded the home price. This age is well within life expectancies, making the odds quite favorable that they could see this outcome with a HECM line of credit. When this happens, there is the potential to obtain a windfall from the line of credit, since it represents a non-recourse loan. This serves as protection, especially when the value of the home declines during retirement.

Exhibit 9.1 Probability that HECM Principal Limit Exceeds the Home Value for a 62-Year-Old

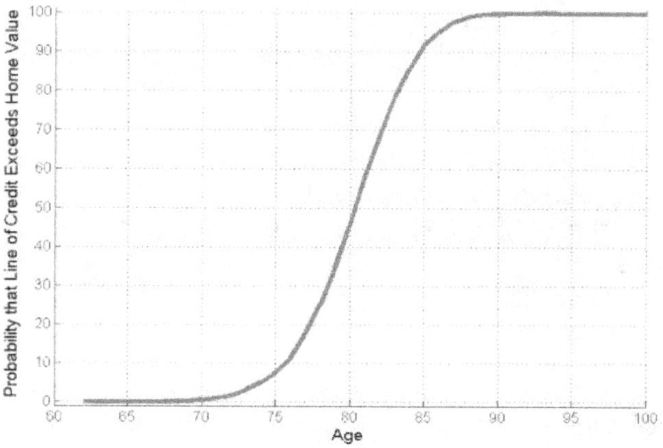

A few caveats are worth discussing with this strategy to hedge home prices with the HECM. First, these probabilities may actually be underestimated because an individual's home will experience more price volatility than the overall Case-Shiller index for home prices. Individual homes will be more at risk of experiencing substantial price declines relative to the index, creating more opportunity for the hedging value to be realized. The line of credit becomes valuable in cases when the home price falls. In the language of financial economics, it is essentially a "put option" on the value of the home. The line of credit can provide a positive net payment when the home value declines.

Second, there is an important aspect of timing the decision about when to access the line of credit. The longer you wait, the greater the potential growth for the pot of funds that can be obtained. Generally, the principal limit, loan balance, and line of credit grow at the same rate. But for any loan balance, the growth reflects the growing interest and mortgage premiums due, rather than growing access to new funds. Waiting is advantageous, but if you wait too long and suddenly die, it's too late and the line of credit is no longer available. Estates and non-borrowing spouses would not be able to take advantage of the windfall after the sudden death of the borrower. It would be best not to become too greedy once a windfall has developed from the non-recourse aspects of the HECM program.

Finally, to be clear, this use of a HECM line of credit as an insurance policy could be considered as a "loophole" in the current program. Opening a reverse mortgage and then not using it works against the interests of some lenders and the government's mortgage insurance fund. The lender is not able to charge interest, which could create real difficulties for lenders who have reduced upfront costs by providing a higher margin and have paid a commission to the loan originator. Also, the mortgage insurance fund is unable to collect further premiums to support their need to cover any shortfall to the lender when the borrower gets more out of the home than it is worth.

With this approach, borrowers may be encouraged in subtle ways to let the value of their home decline so they will be able to make a smaller repayment. Thus, while this option is available today—and I could say it is even encouraged with the heightened government efforts to reduce the speed at which borrowers use up their line of credit—I would expect that the government will eventually work to weaken or eliminate this hedging opportunity.

As new businesses are increasingly able to offer real-time estimates of home value, one possibility for future borrowers is that the borrowing capacity is capped at the appraised home value. Another possibility is that the government could begin to charge the mortgage insurance premium on the value of the principal limit rather than on the loan balance. This would vastly increase the cost of the insurance strategy, possibly overturning its value completely. However, for the time being, these insurance opportunities exist within the current HECM program.

Further Reading

Pfau, Wade D. 2014. "The Hidden Value of a Reverse Mortgage Standby Line of Credit." *Advisor Perspectives* (December 9). [Link]

CHAPTER 10: VALUE OF GOOD FINANCIAL DECISION MAKING IN RETIREMENT

In the previous chapters, I sought to provide context for how a retirement income strategy can extend beyond traditional wealth management to better manage the many risks of retirement. Namely, I discussed a variety of ways a strategic plan for home equity can benefit a retirement income plan.

As we approach the end of this story, this final chapter will turn more toward the process of good financial decision making for retirement and the benefits it can provide to retirees. I will start by explaining more about my own background within the financial services profession, including the roles I play as an educator at The American College of Financial Services and my Retirement Researcher website, and my role in providing financial planning services as a principal at McLean Asset Management.

If you have taken the time to read about how reverse mortgages can fit into a responsible retirement income plan, then you naturally care about this topic. My career decisions do incentivize me to encourage readers to work with financial planners. However, my primary focus is on education, and this is true going back to the days when I started the Retirement Researcher blog while still working as an economics professor in Japan with no connection to the financial services world. I am glad to guide readers toward high quality advisors who can provide net positive impacts on their personal finances. I am also glad to empower and educate readers on how to do this on your own.

I continue the chapter by describing how good decisions impact a financial plan relative to poor decisions. Then I will describe the challenges that we as humans must overcome to make good financial decisions. I have made an effort to provide sufficient information for individuals to construct retirement income plans on their own. However, I recognize that some readers may decide they do not have the time, patience, or inclination to do it all on their own. Thus, I also explain how the financial advisory profession works, and what McLean Asset Management is able to do to help you build an efficient retirement income plan.

How I Fit into the Financial Services Profession

It is worthwhile to explain how I fit into the financial services profession so you can better understand what motivated me to research reverse mortgages in the first place, and then write a book about them.

From 2003 to 2013, I worked as an economics professor in Tokyo, at a university that primarily served graduate students who worked as government officials in developing and emerging market countries. My research during those years centered on public pension systems in countries such as Vietnam, Thailand, and Pakistan. My interest in finance was mostly prompted by managing my own personal finances, and reading books like *A Random Walk Down Wall Street* led me to become a passive investor with a focus on low costs and a long-term mindset.

By 2009, I started to become serious about moving my family back to the United States. I started studying for the CFA examinations in 2009 as a way to make myself more marketable for U.S. employers. In 2010, I had obtained access to a dataset that provided financial market returns from a variety of countries extending back to 1900. I don't recall exactly how I first came across William Bengen's 4% rule for retirement income, but I believe it was mentioned briefly in the CFA curriculum. I thought it could be interesting to see how the 4% rule would have performed in other countries and not just the United States. I finished an article on the topic in September 2010 as my first entry at my new Retirement Researcher blog, and submitted it for review at the *Journal of Financial Planning.*

The article was published in December 2010. For a traditional academic, this publication was remarkable for two reasons. First, publication took place three months after submission, which is extremely fast compared to the academic world where it could take journals one to three years to publish articles. Second, I received reader feedback, indicating that the article was actually being read and not just collecting dust on university library bookshelves. I was hooked and made a full transition from economics to personal financial planning. I published a number of additional research articles about retirement income in the *Journal of Financial Planning* in 2011 and 2012 and even won the journal's award for the most influential article published in 2011, while still living and working in Japan.

The American College of Financial Services

As a part of my ongoing efforts to return to the United States, I interviewed with The American College in August 2012. I accepted an offer to become a Professor of Retirement Income, teaching primarily in the new Ph.D. program on financial and retirement planning, starting in April 2013. The American College was building the Retirement Income Certified Professional (RICP) designation and making the relatively new field of retirement income into a top priority for the future. I believe that my job title at The American College is unique.

Originally created by Solomon Heubner, a University of Pennsylvania professor in the Wharton School who sought to professionalize the life insurance industry, the American College dates back to 1927. The American College created the CLU designation for insurance agents and for many years most of its students were from the insurance industry. In recent years, the American College has expanded to provide education for all of the financial services profession, though the university still carries an aura of being intertwined with the insurance industry, and certainly many of its students and funding comes from the insurance side of financial services profession.

The American College pioneered the RICP designation for financial advisors later in 2012. It provides fair and comprehensive coverage to the different schools of thought and philosophies about retirement income planning, including investments and insurance approaches. I know this because I helped to develop the curriculum. The American College is also one of the leading educators for the CFP program, which historically is connected more to the investments and fiduciary side of the ongoing financial services debate. Today, The American College serves both sides of the financial services profession and seeks to provide ongoing leadership in retirement income planning. Some of my colleagues have become equally intrigued by reverse mortgages, and I hope The American College can become a leading independent resource for information and research about reverse mortgages.

McLean Asset Management

In late 2012, I also began a correspondence with Alex Murguia, who is the CEO of McLean Asset Management, headquartered in McLean, Virginia. At first, he brought me in to work with inStream Solutions, an independent financial planning software company he developed for advisory firms when he was not satisfied with any of the existing financial planning software available for financial advisors. The software can dramatically improve the efficiency of financial advisors and help ensure that all of their clients' financial plans are updated and monitored on a daily basis.

Though inStream is fully independent of McLean, I worked and still work as Director of Retirement Research at the company, having helped build a safe savings rate module, create distribution rules to guide retirement withdrawals, develop ways to compare financial plans with metrics going beyond the simple probability of failure, build reasonable capital market assumptions to guide the Monte Carlo simulations, and implement a Social Security calculator.

As I worked with inStream, I learned more about McLean and came to understand that McLean is a fee-only fiduciary firm that truly understands the retirement income problem. They understand the need to build efficient retirement income strategies that may reduce assets managed in the short-term, but will help their clients the most in the long-term. McLean also shares my interest in education, as Alex holds a Ph.D. himself. In 2014, I joined McLean Asset Management as a principal at the firm. Working with McLean provides the resources to strengthen my Retirement Researcher website and help get my message out to a wider audience, with an understanding that education is the primary goal.

Retirement Researcher

I created my Retirement Researcher blog in September 2010. As my blog has developed over the years, I have still tried to maintain the original mission stated on earlier versions of the site: RetirementResearcher.com provides independent, data-driven, and research-based information about retirement income planning. The website is geared toward providing unbiased information about building efficient retirement income strategies and is willing to cross between the various silos of the financial services profession. I outlined in Chapter 1 how there are two completely different schools of thought about retirement income planning: the probability-based approach and the safety-first approach. My website seeks to provide an understanding about both so readers can better determine the best approach for their personal circumstances, and McLean Asset Management shares this objective with me. Originally, I thought my website would be of most interest for sophisticated consumers who are approaching retirement and have a good understanding of the basics of investments and insurance. But I have found that this education is equally valued by financial advisors, and so my audience is equally split between the two groups.

There are plenty of financial education websites aimed at consumers, but they tackle it from a different angle. My aim is to build a website that empowers readers about retirement income and further expands into other areas important for an effective retirement. The key is to provide readers with a clearinghouse of knowledge, which allows them to take the best of what is empirically valid in a cohesive manner and digest at their own pace what they need. So, let's take a step back from the reverse mortgage topic and seek to better quantify the value of good financial decision making.

The Value of Good Financial Decision Making

Good financial planning decisions extend well beyond where and how you invest. Two major research efforts have attempted to quantify how good financial decision making can enhance your lifetime standard of living. It is important to understand what this research means, because it may not always equal a higher portfolio return in the short term.

The research identifies how good decision making can enhance sustainable lifetime income on a risk-adjusted basis. The ability to spend more than you could have otherwise means your assets are generating a higher net return after accounting for taxes, fees, and good decision making, which makes the higher spending possible.

In the field of finance, the term "alpha" identifies how a fund manager can combine securities into a portfolio that provides excess returns to investors above the appropriate related benchmark for those investments on a risk-adjusted basis. In simple terms, achieving alpha means earning more money than a risk-appropriate index would have provided. Generally, this is achieved through either timing market trends correctly or picking winning individual securities. If a fund manager charges a fee of 1% of assets under management and produces alpha of 2%, the investor enjoys an overall net gain of 1%. After fees, the investor earned 1% more than they would have had they invested directly in the benchmark index.

In practice, it is very difficult to achieve alpha consistently from market timing and security selection, though many investment managers still seem to believe otherwise. Some investment managers are able to beat the market, but it is difficult to separate skill from luck, and even more difficult for those managers to subsequently continue to outperform. The difficulty in generating investment alpha can help explain the rise of indexing in recent years as a more effective alternative. Low cost index funds generally perform better than the majority of actively managed funds, at least after accounting for management fees. As a side note, many readers may not even realize they are paying fees on mutual funds since the fees do not appear on portfolio statements and investors never receive a receipt. It is important to look for the ongoing expense ratio and loads charged at the time of purchase or sale.

After fees, alpha is typically negative for actively managed funds. Mathematically, the average fund must earn the average market return before fees. Some do better and some worse, but the average is the average. After fees, though, the average fund will fall behind the market. Those who understand this point can dramatically simplify their portfolio by filling it with strategic well-diversified, low-cost funds and generally avoiding trading except for rebalancing, tax reasons, or to generate distributions for retirement spending.

In this regard, investing has now mostly been commoditized, at least when investing is done without regard for the overall financial plan. Financial advisors solely focused on selecting investments will struggle to add value for clients. Unfortunately, asset selection is all many advisors do, and the public is often unaware of the existence of advisors who do much more than just manage investments.

Another development from this changing investment world is that for good advisors, investing does not occur in a vacuum. The old investing framework went something like this: "Let's invest, see how it goes, and then determine what you can spend." The new methodology for good advisors is to first figure out what you want to accomplish with your wealth and then build a low-cost strategy to achieve this. Your goals provide the context for how to structure and deploy assets. The structure, process, and ongoing plan adjustment to accommodate life's ever-changing desires and goals becomes the method for adding value to the financial plan.

There is immense value in comprehensive financial planning and good financial decision making. It is important to remember and easy to forget that the end goal of comprehensive financial planning goes beyond choosing investments.

The term "alpha" has been shown to be insufficient when it comes to financial planning, since it only refers to investing in a vacuum. Two articles sought to replace it with a term that represents more than merely beating the market. Vanguard proposes the term "Advisor Alpha" to explain this broader concept. David Blanchett and Paul Kaplan at Morningstar settled on "Gamma." One thing is certain, as it pertains to investing, "alpha" is really just a Greek word for "myth."

Vanguard's Advisor Alpha

Vanguard developed their Advisor Alpha concept in 2001. Their infographics show their overall estimate for Advisor Alpha as 3% on a net basis (4% less an assumed 1% advisory fee). In the introduction of their report, they explain their objective is to shift the focus away from "traditional beat-the-market objectives" (i.e. traditional alpha) toward what they view as the "best practices of wealth management."

These best practices are separated into several categories, shown in Exhibit 10.1, that focus on tax efficiency, costs, risk management, and making good investment decisions.

Suppose a good comprehensive financial advisor who does all these things charges a fee of 1% of assets under management. An investor who can do all of the above on his or her own can keep that fee. However, investors who don't know how to effectively implement everything above—or choose to devote their time and energy elsewhere—miss this extra Advisor Alpha. Even though they saved the 1% fee, they will likely end up worse off for not implementing all of these other important aspects of a good financial plan.

Exhibit 10.1 Components of Vanguard's Advisor Alpha: Impact on an Investor's Returns

1. Build a customized investment plan aimed at achieving goals and meeting constraints for risk tolerance and risk capacity

>0%	Suitable asset allocation with broadly diversified investments
0.45%	Focus on low-cost investments (low expense ratios)
0 – 0.75%	Locating assets properly in taxable and tax-advantaged accounts
>0%	Focusing on total-returns investing instead of income investing

2. Minimize risks and tax impacts

0.35%	Rebalancing to the strategic asset allocation
0 – 0.70%	Deciding where to draw assets from (tax-deferred or taxable) to meet spending

3. Behavioral coaching

> 1.5%	Providing support to stay the course in times of market stress

Overall net impact of good advice: about 3%

Justin Wagner from Vanguard offers the following example for this important point. Suppose the overall market return is 8%. Without good financial decision making, the combined impact of fees, taxes, and poor investment decisions is around 4%. This leaves a net return of 4% to the investor. However, for someone working with a capable advisor, they eliminate poor investment decisions, minimize taxes, and only pay the 1% fee, leaving a net return of 7%. These higher net returns can then be translated into an improved retirement lifestyle and a better ability to meet financial goals. That is the Advisor Alpha. The value added by good advice can greatly exceed the fees, which leaves the investor in a much better position even after paying the advisor. It is incorrect to view advisory fees as a zero-sum game the advisor wins at the expense of the client; both can be winners.

Morningstar's Gamma

David Blanchett and Paul Kaplan at Morningstar created a similar study about the value of good decision making. Their results and approach are different from those of Vanguard, but the goal is the same: to quantify the costs of poor and good decision making. Naturally, many assumptions must be made regarding good financial decisions and the impact of poor financial decisions. The Morningstar research is more directly focused on how retirees can achieve higher income, which they call "gamma." They left out issues like behavioral coaching and included other matters like dynamic retirement spending. Full details can be found in their article, "Alpha, Beta, and Now... Gamma," published in the Fall 2013 issue of the *Journal of Retirement*.

The dimensions for improving financial decisions considered in their article are broken down into several issues, along with consideration of how a naïve investor might approach each issue and how an improved outcome could be achieved with improved knowledge and education, or with the help of a professional.

1. Total Wealth Asset Allocation

The issue: Making asset allocation decisions after considering total wealth including lifetime human capital (future employment earnings).

Naïve investor: Makes asset allocation decisions without considering the role of lifetime human capital.

Improved Outcome: Calculate the present discounted value of lifetime earnings to be saved. Determine the characteristics of lifetime income in terms of whether it is more bond-like or stock-like. Consider this as an asset in your portfolio and then figure out the asset allocation for the financial portfolio in order to obtain the final overall desired asset allocation for wealth.

2. Dynamic Withdrawal Strategy

The issue: Making withdrawal decisions using a variable spending strategy that updates spending to keep a similar probability of failure for the remaining time horizon in retirement.

Naïve investor: Uses the 4% rule: takes out 4% at retirement, then increases that amount by inflation in subsequent years for as long as possible until wealth is depleted.

Improved outcome: Make dynamic decisions based on a circular process. Every year, determine retirement horizon, asset allocation, and maximum withdrawal percentage for a given target probability of failure. Repeat annually to determine spending.

3. Annuity Allocation

The issue: Using product allocation to devote some financial assets to purchasing guaranteed income products may improve outcomes.

Naïve investor: Views annuities as a gamble on dying too soon and ignores them as a retirement income option.

Improved outcome: View annuities as insurance against outliving your wealth by relying on the guaranteed income for life. Allocate part of the financial portfolio to an income annuity at retirement, while also keeping the same overall amount invested in stocks. In other words, part of the allocation to bonds in the retirement portfolio is transitioned into an income annuity.

4. Tax Efficiency Through Asset Location and Withdrawal Sequencing

The issue: Maximizing tax efficiency by locating assets in the most tax efficient places and withdrawing assets in a more tax efficient manner.

Naïve investor: Ignores these issues by keeping the same asset allocation for both tax-deferred and taxable accounts, and then withdraws proportionately from each account in retirement.

Improved outcome: Use efficient asset location by filling tax-deferred accounts with bonds, while stocks would be used in taxable accounts as much as possible. Couple that with efficient withdrawal sequencing, which first spends down taxable accounts, and then move on to tax-deferred accounts.

5. Liability Relative Optimization

The issue: The true risk for a retirement portfolio is not the annual volatility of the asset portfolio, nor is it the performance of the asset portfolio relative to a benchmark. Rather, it is the risk that you won't be able to meet your spending goals.

Naïve investor: Makes asset allocation decisions with no regard for spending goals, focusing instead solely on single-period Modern Portfolio Theory concepts.

Improved outcome: Make investment decisions specifically with spending liabilities in mind. This could result in a portfolio with a lower expected return and/or higher volatility than a more traditional one, but it might do a better job meeting lifetime spending needs. Adding a liability creates a different efficient frontier with portfolios that would have previously seemed suboptimal. For instance, TIPS might not play a role in an assets-only optimization problem, but it might do a better overall job of meeting spending needs, especially in high inflation environments.

6. Social Security Claiming

The issue: Social Security retirement benefits may be claimed between ages sixty-two to seventy, with credits provided for those who delay, yet Americans frequently claim Social Security early.

Naïve investor: Claims Social Security retirement benefits at age sixty-two, as do nearly half of Americans.

Improved outcome: Make joint Social Security claiming decisions based on the potential insurance value of Social Security to provide the most possible lifetime income.

By making these improved financial decisions, retirement income can be increased dramatically. Exhibit 10.2 shows that on a risk-adjusted basis, retirement income is 31.8% higher for the individual making good financial planning decisions relative to someone making naïve planning decisions. How much is this worth in alpha terms? In other words, how much would portfolio returns need to be increased to support a 31.8% larger spending level?

Exhibit 10.2 Components of Morningstar's Gamma

Financial Behavior	Additional Income Generated	Gamma Equivalent Alpha
1. Dynamic Withdrawal Strategy	9.88%	0.70%
2. Total Wealth Asset Allocation	6.43%	0.45%
3. Tax Efficiency	3.23%	0.23%
4. Liability Relative Optimization	1.65%	0.12%
5. Annuity Allocation	1.44%	0.10%
6. Social Security Claiming	9.15%	0.74%
Good Financial Decision Making:	**31.78%**	**2.34%**

Source: Journal of Retirement (Fall 2013) - Factors 1-5; *Journal of Personal Finance* (Fall 2012) - Factor 6

Over a thirty-year period, those starting with a 4% withdrawal rate would need to earn 2.34% more per year as alpha (in the median case)—a difficult task indeed—to increase their income by this amount. This is the "gamma-equivalent alpha." For someone who would otherwise make naïve planning decisions, a 1% advisory fee is worthwhile if that advisor helps the individual make these improved decisions. The net gain to the individual would still be an additional 1.34% in annual market returns, according to the Morningstar research.

Though I use the term "naïve" to describe decisions made without enough attention to good financial planning strategies, it is important to emphasize that many well-informed individuals may fall prey to these decisions. Two things might hold you back: inertia and behavioral finance. It takes discipline to continually make the little adjustments needed to maintain the integrity of the portfolio and subsequent goals. And if you are busy with life, you are probably not going to stay up late on a Wednesday night, for instance, to review/reassess your withdrawal sequencing and asset location. Life can get in the way. It is easy to be an armchair quarterback and think you will not succumb to the naïve decisions because the answers are obvious, but when you are "on the field" that is not always the case.

The Vanguard and Morningstar studies are really just the tip of the iceberg. For instance, ***neither study considered how to incorporate home equity into*** a retirement income plan. We could consider the naïve strategy to be the conventional wisdom of considering a reverse mortgage only as a last resort option in retirement. Chapter after chapter in this book has shown how this is frequently the worst treatment for home equity use.

In addition, these Vanguard and Morningstar studies are naturally

somewhat limited in what they can examine quantitatively. There are many other ways financial advisors may add value which are harder to quantify, such as ensuring you make the right beneficiary designations within an estate plan, are properly insured, and are not missing important strategies to save on taxes. One significant mistake in any of these areas could unravel years of good planning.

In this regard, advisors serve as a type of insurance policy. They provide support to avoid normal life mistakes that come with a lack of experience. Life consists of many economic milestones like retirement, as well as spurious "opportunities" like buying into a time-share, and various potential mistakes driven by behavioral considerations. Working with someone who has seen these situations hundreds of times can be helpful to steer you in the right direction and avoid costly mistakes.

With retirement, it is important to consider how declining cognitive skills associated with aging will make it increasingly difficult to self-manage your investment and withdrawal decisions. For households where one person handles money matters, surviving household members will be especially vulnerable to making mistakes when they outlive the family financial manager. Developing a strong relationship with a trusted financial planner can help with both of these matters.

In terms of cognitive decline, a research article by Michael Finke, John Howe, and Sandra Huston called "Old Age and the Decline in Financial Literacy" outlined the situation well. They provided a financial literacy test to older populations and found that financial literacy tends to decline by about 1% per year after age sixty, but financial confidence remains the same. Other research from David Laibson at Harvard University has also revealed reduced numeracy with age. It becomes harder to perform basic arithmetic calculations and understand the nature of risk, not to mention questions such as which number is smaller: 1/100 or 1/1000?

Can a financial advisor be cost effective? Ultimately, that depends on your answers to a series of important questions:

• Do you have the time, energy, interest, knowledge, and desire to implement all of these decisions on your own? Do you enjoy financial planning?

• Will you overcome the inertia of inaction to put together all the various parts needed to create and implement an effective and coherent overall plan?

• Will you continue to periodically update your plan?

• Have you determined how to make sure your planning will be maintained properly if other family members need to take control of it?

• Are you working with a comprehensive financial planner who does more than just manage investment portfolios and is capable of implementing good financial planning decisions?

Cognitive Decline

Declining abilities to do financial calculations and other types of cognitive impairment make it increasingly difficult to manage a complex investment and withdrawal strategy as you age. It is important to plan ahead and make binding decisions before cognitive impairment sets in. Examples of these binding decisions could include working with a trusted financial planning firm that can be on the lookout for cognitive impairment and help arrange for necessary additional help, or using an income annuity (which David Laibson has called "dementia insurance") to lock in an income stream and reduce the need for portfolio management skills. Since confidence in your financial skills does not decline with age, it is important to plan for these possibilities ahead of time.

If you have the time, interest, energy, knowledge, emotional detachment, and desire to do your financial planning on your own, then you may make an excellent advisor. If your advisor is less than capable, you might be better off saving yourself the fee or taking your business elsewhere. Otherwise, it is worth considering that both of these studies demonstrate how working with a financial advisor can lead to net positive outcomes and be cost effective, especially as you age. It doesn't take much to improve your standard of living through better decision making, even after accounting for any fee related to planning advice.

Behavioral Economics

In the previous section, "behavioral coaching" was suggested to have the biggest impact on real-world investor returns. In Vanguard's analysis, being able to overcome your own behavioral quirks could add more than 1.5% to your returns, as opposed to falling victim to your own human tendencies. If an advisor can successfully provide behavioral coaching to clients, stopping them from both losing their cool and taking drastic, hasty actions in times of market stress, then the outcome can still be a net win for the client after accounting for fees. Even for those who generally always make the right decision regarding their portfolios, a single investment mistake (such as getting out of the stock market in late 2008/early 2009) made near retirement could overturn years of good decision making. The impact of making a wrong financial decision as you get older and/or wealthier becomes harder to overcome. Sequence of returns risk has a corollary here: the timing of mistakes can lead some to have a bigger impact on the lifetime standard of living than others.

To further quantify this matter, Financial Engines published a study in May 2014 with Aon Hewitt that looked at outcomes for defined contribution retirement plan participants between 2006 and 2012. The 30.3% of participants who elected to receive some form of help with their retirement plan on average earned *3.32% more per year,* net of fees, relative to those not receiving investment help. If you have a $1 million portfolio, that's over $30,000 you're leaving on the table. The study also noted that 60.5% of those not receiving help were taking inappropriate amounts of risk, including a large group of near-retirees holding overall portfolios that were more volatile than the S&P 500.

With behavioral coaching being the biggest factor in improving financial outcomes, further exploration is warranted into the types of behaviors that lead investors astray; this can highlight the importance of having someone serve as a sounding board and provide input when working your way through a lifetime of financial decisions. A short introduction to the topic of behavioral finance would be beneficial at this juncture.

Probably the most damaging behavioral mistake made by real-world investors is succumbing to the greed and fear cycle that causes someone to buy into the market at its peak and sell out at its lows. This natural cycle happens thusly: when markets are doing well, investors get excited and pour more money into the market with the hope that this trend will continue indefinitely. Investors on the sidelines may become jealous of neighbors' gains and may worry that they are missing out. But a prolonged run-up generally leads to market valuations becoming misaligned, and it is reasonable to expect a reversal of fortune with lower returns in the future.

Nonetheless, popular culture will send repeated messages that this time is somehow different—it is a new economy with a new paradigm, the old rules no longer apply, and so on. It is tough to rebalance to your strategic asset allocation when markets are rising, because you have to sell shares of the biggest gainers in order to do so. But it is important to have the discipline to stick with your plans and objectives.

A reversal of the market direction is inevitable, causing market prices to plummet. Investors get nervous and some, after seeing significant declines, become scared enough that they start selling off holdings.

Staying the course is an even greater challenge if you are experiencing cognitive decline. Unfortunately, this time in life calls for rebalancing to your strategic asset allocation, which would require buying assets with falling prices rather than selling them. This is a challenge, both emotionally and intellectually.

Exhibit 10.3 Behavioral Cycle of Investing

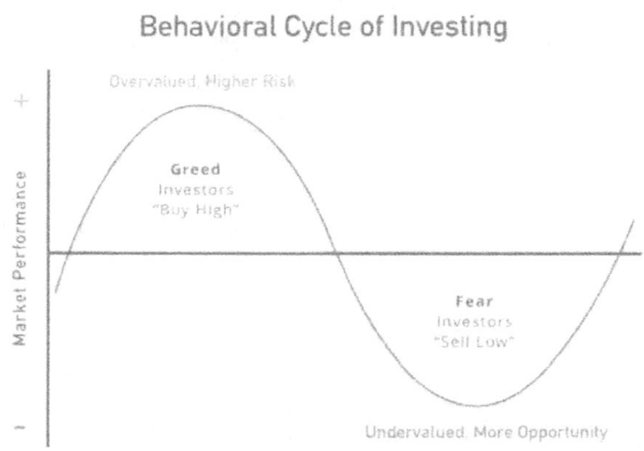

Naturally, weak markets will eventually recover and go up again. However, the timing of the recovery is unpredictable. You cannot time the market. Instead, you must stick with your financial plan and the asset allocation that matches your tolerance for market volatility. Unfortunately, investors in financial markets tend to do the opposite of what happens in most other markets: they buy more when prices are high and sell when prices are low. This causes returns to drag dramatically behind what a "buy, hold, and rebalance" investor could have earned. Staying the course would work better. This is the type of "behavioral coaching" Vanguard refers to in their study.

Why do we as humans need to be coached in our behavior? Evolution has not designed us to be effective long-term investors, but rather to seek to avoid short-term dangers. The fields of behavioral finance and behavioral economics have uncovered various biases humans have which are great for day-to-day survival, but somewhat maladaptive for long-term investing. A significant body of research is dedicated to detailing these investor behaviors.

Some of the most common behaviors an advisor helps individual investors with are:

• Availability Bias/Recency Effect: Using recent or current market behavior to predict future market behavior.

The most recent events are always freshest in our minds, and we tend to extrapolate recent events into the future, expecting more of the same. Large recent market gains lead us to be optimistic about our chances, while market losses have the opposite effect. It takes discipline to overcome these natural tendencies.

• Overconfidence: Believing you know more than other investors.

While investment research increasingly points to the difficulty of beating the market—especially after fees, trading costs, and taxes are taken into account—it is natural to believe we know more than everyone else. This is the "Lake Wobegon effect" in practice. As Garrison Keillor relates in *A Prairie Home Companion,* Lake Wobegon is a place "where all the children are above average." It is all too easy for investors, and even many advisors, to fall into this kind of thinking.

• Loss Aversion: Fearing a loss more than you want to make gains.

As human beings, we tend to feel the pain of experiencing a loss is greater than the joy felt by an equivalent gain. Not recognizing this predisposition can cause people to misjudge their tolerance for risk, making them more likely to bail on their financial plan. Research by Eric Johnson at Columbia University (see the Schlomo Benartzi article for further reading) shows loss aversion is greater among retirees. Johnson found that retirees feel roughly ten times worse about losing $100 than they feel good about gaining $100. Or, more specifically, the retirees in their research said they would not accept a gamble with a 50% chance of winning $100 and a 50% chance of losing $10. The general population is loss averse, but generally not to this extent.

• Hindsight Bias: Thinking you can predict market behavior because you believe you know why past market behavior occurred.

In hindsight, market losses may seem to have an obvious or intuitive explanation. This bias can feed into our overconfidence and cause us to believe we will be able to anticipate such market changes the next time around.

• Survivorship Bias: Underestimating the risk by ignoring the failed companies.

We may underestimate the degree of market risk if we look only at companies still operating today. This misses out on the lessons of many failed companies no longer on the investment radar. It is like thinking a marathon would be easy to run because you watched a bunch of people cross the finish line. You're ignoring all the people who gave up before reaching the end. This can also feed overconfidence.

• Herd Mentality: Judging your own success or failure based on that of others.

Sometimes the herd mentality can be rationalized. You don't want to miss out on being rich when everyone else is rich, and perhaps being poor is not so bad when everyone else is also poor. But for a long-term investor, following the herd rarely makes sense.

• Affinity Traps: Taking advice from someone just because you know them.

We often take the advice of someone simply based on the fact that we like them or share a social circle, regardless of that person's qualifications to speak on investment and personal finance topics.

Further behavioral issues must be considered when it comes to retirement income. Research by Alessandro Previtero at UCLA (see the Schlomo Benartzi article for further reading) shows that recent stock market performance has a big impact on the decision between lump-sum or lifetime income options from pensions. Those making the pension decision after stock market increases over the past six to twelve months are much more likely to select a lump sum instead of guaranteed income, allowing recent market performance to influence this important and irreversible decision. That is recency bias in action.

Research from Jeffrey Brown at the University of Illinois illustrates how the framing of lifetime income can lead to different answers. His research team surveyed more than 1,300 people aged fifty and older and asked them to choose between, (1) a life annuity paying $650 each month until death, or (2) a traditional savings account of $100,000 bearing 4% interest. These choices are designed to support the same lifetime income after incorporating life expectancies, but the annuity choice in option (1) was expressed in two different ways. With a "consumption frame," option (1) was described as a monthly income of $650 for life. With an "investment frame," option (1) was described as an investment with a $650 return for life. When expressed in terms of consumption, 70% of respondents preferred the annuity. But when expressed as an investment, only 21% of respondents choose the annuity. Both versions of the question offer the same returns, but the answers elicited differ greatly. Framing an annuity as an investment makes people worry they will die early and "lose" on their investment. When expressed as lifetime consumption, the annuity option sounds less risky and more attractive.

Further research from Professor John Payne at Duke University (see the Schlomo Benartzi article for further reading) demonstrates how retirees gravitate toward options that are easier to understand. He cites how retirees may choose single-life annuities because they offer higher monthly income than joint-life annuities with fully reflecting on the potential impact for spouses. I have also observed this problem with complex annuities like variable annuities with guarantee riders. Retirees frequently misinterpret the roll-up rates offered for the benefit base as a guaranteed return for their money. They may not realize that when this higher hypothetical return number is combined with a lower payout rate later on, the combined outcome may actually leave them worse off. It's important to dig beyond the marquee numbers jumping out of the marketing literature and reflect on what is truly happening when all variables and levers are combined into a cohesive whole.

A final issue is money illusion: the difficulty people have distinguishing between observable dollar amounts over time and the underlying change in purchasing power of wealth. This can complicate retirement planning, since it is important to plan over long time horizons. Even a low inflation rate adds up when compounded over a long time period.

Understanding How the Financial Advisory Profession Works

With the value provided by good financial decision making, and the impediments people face to achieve good financial outcomes for themselves, it is worthwhile discussing more about the advisory profession. How can you find a good advisor?

Though the financial services profession is highly regulated at both the state and national levels, use of the terms "financial advisor" or "financial planner" as job titles is hardly regulated. Regulation generally focuses on the nature of business activities rather than job titles. Pretty much anyone can use these terms without any further oversight about training, competency, education, or qualifications.

Generally, those calling themselves financial planners or advisors represent one of three types: registered investment advisors, stock brokers, or insurance agents.

Of the three types, investment advisors are the only ones required to serve as fiduciaries for their clients, at least when they are wearing their "investment advisor" hat. The fiduciary standard of care requires investment advisors to act in the best interests of clients and disclose any material conflicts of interest to clients for the advice they provide. Fiduciary advisors who serve only as fiduciary advisors are generally part of Registered Investment Advisor (RIA) firms, and they often use the term "fee only" to differentiate themselves from competitors. The National Association for Personal Financial Advisors (NAPFA) is the membership organization for fee-only advisors. A fee-only advisor is paid directly and only by their clients, generally as a percentage of assets the advisor manages. That percentage generally decreases as the account size increases. Fees usually cover financial planning advice and investment management.

Some fee-only advisors may have different fee structures. Other possibilities include an hourly charge or fixed retainer fees for services. With other fee arrangements, the advisor is less likely to make trades on their client's behalf. With such fee arrangements, the advisor makes investment recommendations but the client implements them.

The important point of this fee structure, and the meaning of "only" within the term "fee only," is that these advisors are paid only by their clients. They do not receive any commissions or other financial incentives for getting their clients into any particular investments or financial products, which eliminates an obvious source of potential conflicts. A comprehensive financial planner should assist their clients with eight core planning areas: investments, taxes, debt management, education planning, retirement planning, estate planning, insurance, and household budgeting.

As you can see, there is much to do beyond just investment management. Presently, the fiduciary standard of care is not applied to brokers or insurance agents, though new rules from the Department of Labor in April 2016 could substantially change the advisory landscape. The Department of Labor enacted rules to strengthen requirements for those advising on retirement plans to serve as fiduciaries. These landmark rule changes could have big impacts over the coming years, since retirement plan assets represent a significant portion of the investment assets held by American households.

Presently, brokers and insurance agents are treated more generally as salespeople, and they are required to use a suitability standard of care with their customers. Any recommended financial products must be "suitable" for the purchaser's situation, though the recommendations do not necessarily need to serve the best interests of the purchaser. For those acting as brokers and insurance agents, their primary professional obligation is to their employer rather than their client. For instance, a suitable investment or insurance product that pays a higher commission to the broker or agent—presumably because it is a more profitable product for the employer—could be recommended under the suitability standard, even if another approach would better serve the customer's interests. Surveys of the public generally reveal that most people do not understand the distinctions between the fiduciary and suitability standards, nor do they understand the differences between investment advisors and brokers. Perhaps a simple example is the analogy of selling cars. When you go to a Honda dealership, you reasonably expect the salesperson to sell you a Honda. The salesperson will probably not suggest that you would be better served by heading over to an unaffiliated Ford dealership.

Consumers understand this about people who sell cars, but they often do not recognize that this same issue exists for brokers and agents. People naturally tend to believe financial advisors are independent and seek to work in their clients' best interests, as they should. A fiduciary investment advisor faces little to no conflict in directing client investments because his or her compensation is not tied to a specific product. They can essentially recommend you buy the most fitting car from any available car dealership, which is the treatment consumers generally expect from all advisors. But brokers do not have this freedom; they are obligated to sell their sponsoring company's financial products. If another dealership would fit your needs better, they would still encourage you to buy from them instead.

To make matters worse, low-cost products that can better serve consumers carry a lower commission, making them less desirable for brokers to sell. Products that are harder to sell because of their complexity may have reduced effectiveness for clients, but they tend to carry higher commissions in order to incentivize their sale. It's like doctors providing prescriptions based on pharmaceutical company kickbacks rather than the patient's health.

Many advisor websites make it difficult to understand how they are registered and what sort of standard of care they provide. It would be simple if we could just separate the advisors from the brokers, but a number of advisors are registered as investment advisors and brokers or agents. Dual registration muddles the situation for clients further, as it may not always be clear when the advisor is wearing the hat of a fiduciary, and when they are making recommendations under suitability requirements. Because they can also receive commissions, such dually registered advisors should use the term "fee-based" to describe their firms, rather than "fee-only." However, I'm not sure if all advisors make this distinction for the two terms. Clients could then have a clear understanding of when they are being served under the fiduciary or suitability standard.

Further Reading

Agarwal, Sumit, John C. Driscoll, Xavier Gabaix, and David Laibson. 2009. "The Age of Reason: Financial Decisions Over the Lifecycle and Implications for Regulation." Brookings Papers on Economic Activity 2: 51-117.

Aon Hewitt and Financial Engines. 2014. "Help in Defined Contribution Plans: 2006 through 2012." [Link]

Benartzi, Schlomo. 2010. "Behavioral Finance and the Post-Retirement Crisis." [Link]

Blanchett, David. 2012. "When to Claim Social Security Benefits." Journal of Personal Finance 11:2 (Fall): 36-87.

Blanchett, David, and Paul Kaplan. 2013. "Alpha, Beta, and Now... Gamma." Morningstar Working Paper. Also Published in the Journal of Retirement (Fall 2013). [Link]

Brown, Jeffrey R., Jeffrey R. Kling, Sendhil Mullainathan, and Marian V. Wrobel. 2008. "Why Don't the People Insure Late Life Consumption? A Framing Explanation of the Under-Annuitization Puzzle." NBER Working Paper. [Link]

Finke, Michael S., John S. Howe, and Sandra J. Huston. 2011. "Old Age and the Decline in Financial Literacy." SSRN Working Paper #1948627 (August 24)

Johnson, Richard. W., Cori E. Uccello, and Joshua H. Goldwyn. 2003. "Single Life vs Joint and Survivor Pension Payout Options: How do Married Retirees Choose?" Urban Institute. Final Report to the Society of Actuaries and the Actuarial Foundation.

Kinniry, Francis M., Colleen M. Jaconetti, Michael A. DiJoseph, and Yan Zilbering. 2014. "Putting a Value on Your Value: Quantifying Vanguard Advisor's Alpha." Vanguard Research Paper. [Link]

Murguia, Alex. "What McLean Can Do For You." McLean E-book Series. [Link]

GLOSSARY OF ACRONYMS

- AARP - American Association of Retired Persons
- AGI - Adjusted Gross Income
- ALF - Assisted Living Facility
- CCRC - Continuing Care Retirement Community
- CD - Certificate of Deposit

- CEO - Chief Executive Officer
- CFP - Certified Financial Planner
- CLU - Chartered Life Underwriter
- DIA - Deferred Income Annuities
- FHA - Federal Housing Authority
- FPA - Financial Planning Association
- HECM – Home Equity Conversion Mortgage
- HELOC - Home Equity Line of Credit
- HUD - Department of Housing and Urban Development
- IRA - Individual Retirement Account
- IRS - Internal Revenue Service
- LESA - Life Expectancy Set-Aside
- LIBOR - London Interbank Offered Rate
- LOC - Line of Credit
- MIP - Mortgage Insurance Premium
- MPT - Modern Portfolio Theory
- NAPFA - National Association for Personal Financial Advisors
- PLF - Principle Limit Factor
- RIA – Registered Investment Adviser
- RICP - Retirement Income Certified Professional
- SPIA - Single-Premium Immediate Annuities
- TIPS - Treasury Inflation-Protected Securities

www.ingramcontent.com/pod-product-compliance
Lightning Source LLC
LaVergne TN
LVHW022059200926
848481LV00003B/982
* 9 7 8 1 8 0 7 6 5 0 5 1 3 *